THE SPIRAL OF TIME SERIES

RAV DOVBER PINSON

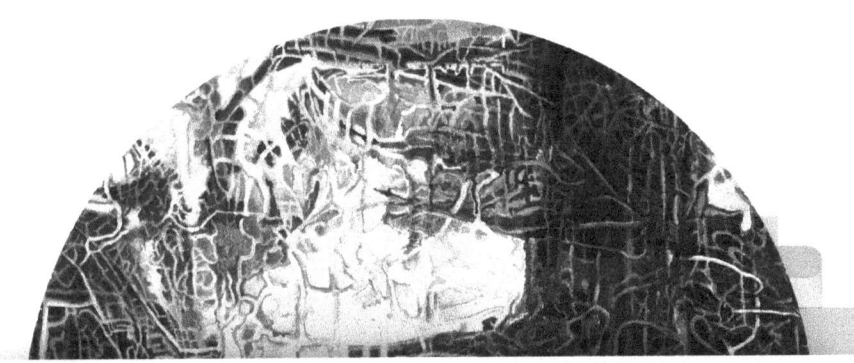

THE MONTH of TEVES

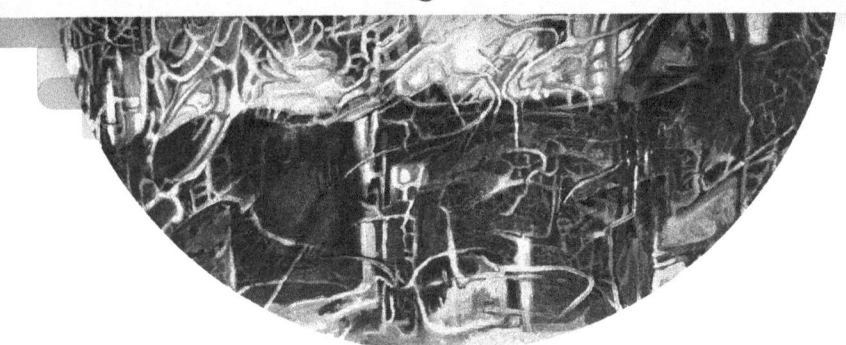

vol **10**

◆• REFINING RELATIONSHIPS | ELEVATING THE BODY •◆

IYYUN PUBLISHING

THE MONTH OF TEVES © 2018 DovBer Pinson. All rights reserved. No part of this book may be used or reproduced in any manner whatsoever without written permission except in the case of brief quotations embodied in critical articles and reviews.

Published by IYYUN Publishing
232 Bergen Street
Brooklyn, NY 11217

http:/www.iyyun.com

Iyyun Publishing books may be purchased for educational, business or sales promotional use. For information please contact: contact@IYYUN.com

Editor: Reb Matisyahu Brown

Developmental Editor: Reb Eden Pearlstein

Proofreading: Alyssa Elbogen

Proofreading / Editing: Simcha Finkelstein

Cover and book design: RP Design and Development

Cover image: "Conserve the Destruction" by Kalam Shamsudin

pb ISBN 9780989007252

Pinson, DovBer 1971-
The Month of Teves: Refining Relationships, Elevating the Body
1.Judaism 2. Jewish Spirituality 3. General Spirituality

vol **10**

THE MONTH *of* TEVES

◆• REFINING RELATIONSHIPS | ELEVATING THE BODY •◆

IYYUN PUBLISHING

DEDICATION

In honor of

ראובן ומרים
Miriam & Richard Friedman שיחי'

*May they continue to experience
pure nachas and joy
from their children, grandchildren
and great-grandchildren,
in perfect health and prosperity.*

CONTENTS

2 | OPENING

5 | THE MONTH OF TEVES: An Overview

17 | PERMUTATION OF HASHEM'S NAME

21 | TORAH VERSE

24 | LETTER

31 | NAME OF THE MONTH

37 | SENSE

49 | SIGN

55 | TRIBE

59 | BODY PART

68 | ELEMENT

70 | TORAH PORTIONS

74 | SEASON OF THE YEAR

80 | THE HOLIDAY OF THE MONTH

85 | PRACTICE

99 | SUMMARY OF TEVES

104 | APPENDIX A:
Five Levels of Relationship

111 | APPENDIX B:
The Tenth of Teves: The Beginning of all Exiles

OPENING

*E*ACH MONTH OF THE YEAR RADIATES WITH A DISTINCT quality and provides unique opportunities for personal growth and illumination. Accordingly, every month has a slightly different climate and represents a particular stage in the 'story of the year' as expressed through the annual cycles of nature. The winter months call for practices and pursuits that are different than those of the summer months. Some months are filled with holidays and some have only one, or none. Each month therefore has its own natural and spiritual signature.

According to the deeper levels of the Torah, each month's distinct qualities, opportunities and natural phenomena correspond to a certain set of seasonal and spiritual variables arranged within a twelve-part symbolic structure. The spiritual nature of each month is therefore articulated according to its unique entries for each of these twelve categories which include 1) a permutation of G-d's four-letter name, 2) a verse from the Torah, 3) a letter of the Aleph Beis, 4) the name of the month itself, 5) an experiential "sense", 6) a Zodiac sign, 7) a tribe of Israel, 8) a body part, 9) an element, 10) a unit of successive Torah portions that are read during the month, 11) a season of the year, and 12) the holidays or significant events that occur during the month.

By reflecting on these twelve themes and categories, an ever-ascending spiral of insight, understanding and practical action becomes revealed. Learning to navigate and harness the nature of change by consciously engaging with the cycles of time, adds a deeper sense of purpose and heightened presence to our lives.

The present volume will delve into the spiritual nature of the month of Teves according to these twelve categories.

NOTE: *For a more comprehensive treatment of this twelve-part system and the overarching dynamics of the "story of the year," an in-depth introduction has been provided in Volume One of this series, The Spiral of Time: Unraveling the Yearly Cycle.*

4 | THE MONTH OF TEVES

The Month of Teves

When we think of the month of Teves (which usually starts near the beginning of January), the images that come to mind are of long, cold, dark winter nights, and restless days of hunkering down indoors, close to a source of heat. Indeed, Teves is normally the coldest month of the yearly cycle with the shortest time of daylight. It is thus considered a 'harsh' month, due to the stultifying conditions.

This is one way that Teves is a mirror of Tamuz, the 'harsh' month that occurs at the hottest period of the summer. Both months are times of potential negativity. Both have extreme weather, which is but a seasonal expression of the spiritual extremes and harshness manifesting in the world at these times.

In the sequence of the fall and winter months, first comes the month of Tishrei, when we inaugurate a new year with solemnity and festivity, with Rosh Hashanah, Yom Kippur and the joyful holiday of Sukkos. Then comes the rainy month of Cheshvan, a time we yearn to be alone with ourselves, thus beginning a period of 'hibernation', as it were. Cheshvan is *Chash* / quiet, it is a month without holidays or special observances that take us away from being alone. After Cheshvan comes the month of Kislev, in which our aloneness gradually begins to feel lonely, stimulating an urge within us to reconnect with others. Toward the end of Kislev is the festival of Chanukah, a time of family celebration. Just as a small amount of oil lasted for eight days, the small glimmer of light that we actively kindle during Chanukah begins to enter back into our homes in order to grow and become established within our consciousness. After Kislev comes Teves. As the glow of Chanukah continues to grow, we begin to 'see' others around us in a new light, so to speak. Thus, as this month arrives, we seek to find or rediscover intimacy with others by forging deeper relationships outside ourselves.

Throughout the Northern hemisphere, in the bitter cold of Teves we naturally seek the physical closeness and warmth of intimacy. This very natural feeling is predicated and founded on the inner spiritual quality that exists in this month. [Torah thought on the seasons is based exclusively on the Northern Hemisphere, since most Jews lived there throughout history, and most importantly, because it is the location of the Land of Israel.]

Tekufas Teves / the season of Teves ushers in the beginning of the three winter months. As explored in greater depth in *The Spiral of Time*, the year can be subdivided into two parts. The six fall and winter months, when the daylight is diminished, are connected with the paradigm of 'the receiver', represented by the human reality 'below'. During this time the Light from Above is gradually diminished. This is in contrast to the paradigm of the six spring and summer months. The luminosity of this season is connected to 'the Giver', represented by the Divine reality Above. The three months of winter — Teves, Shevat, and Adar — are therefore specifically associated with the body, which is the earthly vessel and receiver of the Heavenly soul. During this time we are particularly focused on our physical needs and functions, and their spiritual correspondences.

Three Archetypal Appetites:

There are three basic needs of the body. The first is the need to perpetuate the body's genetic script through procreation. This urge is connected with the month of Teves, as it is thematically connected with physical intimacy, as we will explore. The second need, eating, is related to the month of Shevat, the month of the New Year of Fruit Trees. Shevat is thus a period conducive to making a *Tikkun* / rectification on our eating and digestion. The need to drink is appropriately associated with the month of Adar, the month of the holiday of Purim, the day on which there is a Mitzvah to drink extra wine.

These three bodily needs must be actively fulfilled, as distinct from other important physical needs such as breathing and sleeping, which are fulfilled passively. That is, even if you do not want to, you will eventually have to breathe and you will eventually fall asleep. Most people simply cannot function without sleeping for three days, so the body will naturally fall asleep on its own [*Shavuos* 25a]. Procreation, eating and drinking, however, are not automatic, they must therefore be consciously engaged.

All living beings eat, drink and procreate. In fact, these primal activities are what define basic animal life: actively seeking food and hydration, which then provide the strength not only to survive but to actively seek mates and procreate. Human beings, when living solely from the place of our animal instincts and neglecting our capacity to consciously choose our course of action, can distort or misappropriate the natural expressions of these three needs. A) In place of true intimacy, the need to procreate can become a drive for shallow pleasure, possessiveness, ego and anger. B) In place of healthy nourishment, the need to eat can become a drive for gluttony and obsession. C) In place of healthy and joyful drinking, the need to imbibe liquids can become an abusive drive for drunkenness and negative self-doubt.

Each of these concepts is explored in its respective volume. The text on Shevat explores the fact that when the intensity of the cold is slightly lessened, people more readily indulge in food which can lead to gluttony. This is one reason that Shevat is a period well-suited for focusing and making a Tikkun on our eating. The text on Adar, the final month of the winter, explores the positive connections between drink, laughter and happiness, offering a proactive Tikkun for any residual self-doubt or tendency toward substance addiction.

As Teves is the coldest, grayest month of the year, we naturally spend more time indoors. In contrast to the previous month of

Kislev, we tend to want to spend this time indoors with others. It is thus a time of reconnection and relationship. It is therefore referred to as a *Yerech sheNeheneh Guf min haGuf* / "a month in which a body takes pleasure from the (warmth of another) body" [*Megilah*, 13a]. This budding desire for physical closeness, which is experienced as a pronounced awakening of the appetites of the physical body and its draw towards intimacy during this month, is certainly not meant to reinforce our egoic attachments to selfish pleasure or reinforce our purely self-serving narratives. It is rather a time to refine and balance these energies and urges in order to hareness and direct them towards health and holiness. For it goes without saying that when physical desires are not channelled or fulfilled in conscious and compassionate ways, they can indeed become catalysts for destructive actions and emotions including anger and self-loathing.

As mentioned, Teves follows Kislev. In Kislev, the first glimmer of growing light on the horizon corresponds to the inner light of hope that returns after the winter solstice. Although we are very much affected by the cold and seeming deadness of winter, the subtle and gradual return of sunlight stimulates a renewed feeling of hope within us, prompting us to reach outside of ourselves and reconnect with others in meaningful relationships. While Kislev, following the solitary 'hibernation' of Cheshvan, opens us up to the possibility of reconnecting with other people, now, in Teves, we are more actively working on deepening those interpersonal relationships. However, since there is a very strong orientation to the body during the winter months, and because the body is naturally self-centered, it is very important to actively work on redirecting our physical needs and appetites towards positive and productive ends during this time. If you work earnestly and diligently on lessening the ego's natural proclivity towards selfishness, you can consciously craft a meaningful life in which your physical needs do not necessarily lead you to merely receive for yourself, but rather inspire you to become an actual giver in all of your relationships, as well.

Correspondingly, as we work on making a necessary Tikkun and effect a positive re-alignment in our personal relationships, we can also rectify our relationship to the entire physical world, as well as the Divine. By transforming any tendency we may have toward selfishness, possessiveness or anger in the realm of intimate relationships, we may thereby evolve all of our interactions with people and things, as intimacy is the *Yesod* / foundation of all our relationships. As we delve deeper into the spiritual, seasonal, and cosmic qualities of this month, we will learn what we can do to effectively create these Tikkunim. We will also learn how to take advantage of the special energies that are available during Teves to make our lives more joyful, purposeful, and productive.

Teves & Tohu:

For reasons we will explore throughout this text, Teves relates to the very physical, existential, immediate, and even impatient or angry qualities of *Tohu* / chaos — characterized by the qualities of Eisav / Esau. In contrast, Esau's twin brother Yaakov / Jacob embodies the qualities of Tikkun: patience, order, interdependence, healthy boundaries, and respect for individuality (one's own as well as that of others).

What is Tohu? Certainly, this is a far-reaching question that has numerous cosmological and psychological implications, a full treatment of which would require a book of its own. However, for the purposes of our current inquiry into the nature of the month of Teves, we will supply a highly condensed response based on the traditional sources.

In short: In the beginning of creation there was (and of course there still is) only the *Ein Sof* / the Infinite Light of Hashem. In order to create space for a finite existence to manifest, the Infinite Light metaphorically withdrew within itself in an act of *Tzimtzum* / constriction, creating a *Chalal Hapanui* / vacant space, that allowed for the Ten *Sefiros* / Divine attributes (which were already 'hidden' within the Ein Sof) to emerge.

At this stage, the Ten Sefiros then existed as individual points, in a paradigm called 'spotted' or dotted reality, meaning a world with sharp distinctions and clearly defined individuality. Here, in this phase of creation, each of these Ten Attributes sensed its own self-importance, and therefore remained aloof and apart from the other nine. As the Infinite withdrew further within Itself, each emergent 'dot' seized the opportunity to express itself more fully, without regard to the other nine attributes which were simultaneously also self-expressing.

Thus, a cacophony ensued, with all aspects of creation working at cross-purposes with every other aspect. This created a paradigm of competition rather than collaboration. Accordingly, this was a world of strong *Yeshus* / ego, and thus it was perpetually in a condition of *Tohu* / chaos and constant conflict. Again, although the above events are described as a narrative that occurred in the past, this paradigm is also timelessly present as a potential layer within the constantly unfolding process of Creation. As such, this state of self-centered clashing can emerge within one's own life, or within the life of the collective, at any point in which the self sees itself as sovereign, rather than as a servant of something bigger than itself. This is a classic case of a part mistaking itself for the whole, something the ego is naturally inclined to do if left unchecked.

In summary: The Spiritual World of Tohu is where every Divine attribute senses its own self-importance, and therefore remains apart from the others. Each Attribute expresses itself fully, which on some level is a positive thing, however, their individual expression occurs without regard for the existence and importance of the others, which is ultimately what leads to the ensuing chaos and conflict.

As the Creation process matures, the world of Tohu gives way to the deeper world of Tikkun, where each of the ten attributes grow beyond themselves in order to form meaningful bonds with each other. This is accompanied by a corresponding realization that each individual is actually a part or a larger whole; this realization reorients one's awareness beyond the self. Abandoning the self completely is not the goal, however, integrating the self within the context of a larger community does offer the individual the impetus for its next phase of evolution. This cosmic pattern of Tohu-then-Tikkun is also reflected in the general pattern of child development. We all begin life in the world of Tohu and hopefully, gradually, we are able to work our way up and out into the wider world of Tikkun.

Certainly, for the first few years of life we are all in a state of Tohu; we are both filled with chaos, and we are also a source of chaos for others.

Tohu is thus represented by the raw energy of children, who validly need to indiscriminately express their needs and desires. If a child does not cry, how would we know it is hungry or tired? Additionally, when a child feels overlooked or ignored, during adult conversation for example, they may start screaming or making a mess. The moment they receive the attention they crave, they grab center stage and try to steal the show. In such an instance, all the child is doing is protecting his still fragile ego, a developmentally appropriate instinct.

Necessarily, children inhabit this world of self-absorption and Tohu for the first few years of their lives. There is no room for sharing toys or for understanding others, as it is all they can do to learn to understand themselves. As children realize they are actually their own distinct being, separate from their mother, they feel a need to spread themselves over as many things as possible, and claim everything in sight as their own. At this stage, they have not yet realized that just as they are their own unique beings, so is everyone else. However necessary this process of individuation may be, if such behavior were to continue past this developmental stage, if the ego were to never be checked or counterbalanced by the acknowledgement of others outside the self, it would ultimately cause an external and internal meltdown and state of conflict.

In any case, a person must travel a long way before they reach the maturity of the World of Tikkun, which is characterized by harmony, collaboration and interconnectivity. Tikkun is thus where each Divine attribute, each part, allows the other to express itself in the context of a larger, more inclusive whole. In this realm, there is humility, patience and an attenuation of ego.

Tohu and Instant Gratification:

As Tohu is primarily defined and motivated by the unconscious urges of the ego, it is also completely focused on the 'now', constantly seeking instant gratification within the immediate experience. This raw energy is felt and expressed within the physical instincts of the body.

Whereas Tikkun is order, balance and level-headedness, Tohu is imbalanced passion and unbridled desire and energy. Tohu is like the consciousness of a child who wants their toys or ice cream and wants them immediately. The ego of Tohu is acute and all-consuming. It wants things *now*, and at any cost. In the Torah, the patient and strategic Yaakov embodies Tikkun and his brother Eisav, who is passionate and wild, embodies Tohu.

For instance: when Eisav once came home after hunting, he was terribly hungry. He saw that Yaakov had just cooked a bowl of lentils, and he demanded that Yaakov feed him: "Quick! Let me have some of that red stew! I'm famished!" [*Bereishis*, 25:30]. When Yaakov proposed that he exchange his birthright and blessing of the first born for the bowl of stew, Eisav responded, "Look, I am about to die! What good is the birthright to me?" [*Ibid*, 25:32]. Eisav wants the food right away, to the extent that he does not take the future into consideration. His physical appetite overwhelms his spiritual consciousness. Eisav is all about 'right now' — immediate relief, gratification and success — at the expense of his future. Eisav is the type of person who would choose to sacrifice himself for a single battle, even if it meant he would lose the overall war.

Yaakov knows all this and responds, "Sell to me *like the day*... swear to me *like the day*." In this context, Yaakov's phrasing is very intentional. "The day" or 'today', is, again, the moment, the immediately tangible feelings. According to the Zohar [*Zohar Chadash*, Bereishis, 14:1. *Megaleh Amukos,* Toldos], Eisav is likened to the sun and Yaakov to the moon. The sun represents predictability, pure projection, and the need for immediately tangible physical results; the moon on the other hand, represents possibility, process, reflection, and dreams of the future.

An immature child in a candy store stuffs himself with candy and does not think about how he is going to feel sick in an hour. He is too overwhelmed with desire in the moment to think about future consequences. This describes the raw energy of Teves, when left unchecked: brute, passionate, powerful and 'today'.

However, it is also important to note that there is also something special and wonderful about the raw energy of Tohu; it is very passionate and real, much like the sincere excitement and joy of a child digging into a dish of ice cream. Such a child fully relishes their experience, a quality that is often lost as one grows older and more anxious about their future. And so the month of Teves is not only about fixing and creating a Tikkun for Tohu or taming it. While we certainly do need to take time in this month to become more conscious and try to behold the bigger picture of our lives, on another level, in Teves we need to learn to harness and utilize the energy of Tohu as it is for positive ends.

Since the quality of the month is generally harsh — much like its counterpart Tamuz in the summer, the tendency for many is to hunker down, retract, curl up and wait for the month to pass by, only to reemerge when the harshness has dissipated. Think for a moment about the 'easier' months of the year, which, like gentle waves in the ocean, carry us where we want to go. We can ride these energies easily and they can propel us forward effortlessly, we just need to go with the overall flow, so to speak. The harsher months, on the other hand, can be compared to the more powerful waves that emanate from the belly of the ocean, which come forcefully crashing down and can easily drown a person before they even realize what has happened. However, those who want to utilize the momentum of the powerful energy that is available during such times can, with caution and creativity, harness these intense waves and ride them higher and farther than other, more gentle circumstances may allow. However, harnessing the power of Tohu, the raw energy of the body, does in fact need to be approached with great care and attention.

In general, Teves is connected to the body and heat, as we will continue to explore below. It is also associated with the bodily sensations of anger — the raw phenomena of an elevated heart rate, rise in temperature, shortness of breath, and muscular tension. Additionally, this month is also connected with the liver, an organ which is full of blood. All of this imagery expresses the gestalt of this month: an overwhelming sense of the visceral immediacy and raw energy of our physical urges and emotional needs.

PERMUTATION OF HASHEM'S NAME

THE FOUR LETTER ESSENTIAL NAME, YUD-HEI-VAV-HEI (Hashem), is the Divine Source of all Reality. The last three letters of the Name, Hei-Vav-Hei, create the word *Hoveh* / is. The root of this verb means, 'to bring into being'. The first letter of the Name, Yud, serves as a prefix to the last three letters: *Yud-HoVeH*. In this way, the Yud modifies the verb to represent a perpetual activity [see *Iyov*, 1:5]. In other words, the Divine Name can be understood to mean, 'That Which is Continuously Bringing Being into Being'.

For numerous reasons, this Essential Name cannot be spoken. Therefore a common practice is to rearrange its four letters into an alternate construction that may be pronounced. This produces the word HaVaYaH, which literally means 'Being-ness'. This aspect of the Name refers to the Ultimate Being, which is the Source and Substance of all that is. The Ultimate Being does not depend on anything else to exist. It gives rise to all past, present and future manifestations, thereby bringing all things into existence ex nihilo, i.e. *Yesh meAyin* / being from non-being. Accordingly, the individual words for was / *Havah*, is / *Hoveh*, and will be / *Yihyeh*, are all encoded within the Essential Name itself.

As mentioned, Hashem, the Essential Four-Letter Name, is the Source of all Being and Time, and thus is *connected* to actual time. Because of this, each unique period in time is imbued with a special connection to the Essential Name. In terms of the months, this energy is expressed through a unique permutation of the four letters that comprise the Essential Name. Therefore, each month has an inner light that 'shines' through the 'prism' of a different permutation of the four letters of the Name. Each permutation communicates a different spiritual dynamic which is part of the Divine signature encoded within that particular month.

The sequence of the four letters in Hashem's name which corresponds to the month of Teves is Hei-Yud-Hei-Vav. Yud and Vav are in the form of a point and a line respectively (י and ו), representing the masculine, 'giving' aspects of the Name. The letter Hei (ה), which is a wider, more open and multi-dimensional letter, represents the feminine, receptive aspects of the Divine Name.

Any given sequence of the letters depicts a pattern of flow between the Mashpiah or 'giving' letters, and the Mekabel or 'receiving letters'. The flow of the Name in this month is, in a sense, the reverse of the natural order, which generally flows from giver to receiver: it starts with a Mekabel (Hei) below and moves up to a Mashpiah (Yud) above, and then again from another Mekabel (Hei) below to a Mashpiah (Vav) above. This signifies that there is very little revelation flowing 'down' into the world at this time; in other words, there are few 'revealed' blessings in this month. Hei alludes to the world of Asiyah / our dense physical plane of reality. The strong influence of the letter Hei in this month draws our focus toward the physical body and material concerns. Furthermore, since there is very little initiative on the side of the 'giving' letters, as the movement of energy is rooted in and initiated by the 'receivers', Teves is called a 'closed' month, a period in which people tend to be more possessive.

However, there are certainly great hidden blessings available in Teves, and throughout this text, we will learn how to find them and unveil them in our lives. For now, notice that the letter sequence of Hei-Yud-Hei-Vav displays a tendency toward upward developmental movement — from a Hei to the Yud, and a Hei to the Vav. This means there is still a possibility for spiritual elevation and evolution when we realign our physical desires with the Divine purpose within creation.

Appropriately, this month's sequence of the four letters describes the experiential timeline of the month. The first portion of the month is described by the movement from Hei to Yud. Yud symbolizes a revelation from Above, and specifically a manifestation of miracles from the *Ein Sof* / Infinite Light and potential. This is the powerful influence of the final two days of Chanukah, which are the first two days of Teves. The rest of the month is then described by the movement from Hei-to-Vav, as we attempt to shift our spiritual posture from self-centered 'receiver' to compassionate 'giver'. Since the energy of the 'giver' is couched in the dynamic of 'taking' during this month, as evidenced in the repetition of the movement from Hei to Yud or Vav, a quality of selfishness can impact our ability to connect with or relate to others, if not checked and transformed.

TORAH VERSE

THE FOUR LETTER DIVINE NAME THAT SHINES DURING each month is rooted within a particular verse in the Torah [*Tikunei Zohar, Hakdamah* 9b. *Eitz Chayim, Sha'ar* 44:7]. In other words, there is a 'verse of the month' comprised of a four-word sequence, in which each word either begins or ends with the letters of the *Tziruf* / name-formation for that month. In fact, the order of the Tziruf follows the corresponding verses [*Mishnas Chasidim*, Meseches Adar, 1:3]. The meaning and context of the verse connected with each particular month is, of course, also part of the revelation of that month's guiding light.

The permutation of the Divine Name that we explored above comes from the last letters of the verse, *leHavayaH ItiY uNiromemaH ShemO* / "Hashem is with me and thus I exalt His name...." [*Tehillim,* 34:4]. Exaltation or praise, as expressed in this verse, is an expression of profound acknowledgment and appreciation for the presence and being of an other. The state of consciousness from which exaltation or praise flows is quite literally the opposite of self-centeredness, and thus it serves to open up channels of more meaningful communication and connection with people in our lives.

"Exalting" or praise, as expressed in this verse, is the opposite of possessiveness, and it counteracts negative relationships with the people in our lives. Therefore, to "exalt" is a perfect Tikkun for this month. Part of 'praise' is gratitude for what one has. When we are truly thankful for what we have, we are less attached and possessive about it. Being grateful implies that we recognize that what we do have is a gift and not an inevitability or something that is owed to us. This verse empowers us to be thankful, to avoid taking for grant the people in our lives, and to actively affirm praises of Hashem for all the gifts in our lives. The word that follows the four words specified is *Yachdav* / together, alluding to intimacy or unity and harmony with others.

Teves begins with the last few days of Chanukah, which are in general called days of *Hallel veHodaah* / praise and gratitude [*Shabbos,* 21b]. Therefore, on the very first days of this month we recite the Full Hallel, which immediately puts us on the right track to actively elevate ourselves by counteracting the seasonal pull towards egoism. When we praise Hashem, we, who are naturally 'receivers', are, in effect, giving to the ultimate 'Giver'. This 'anti-gravity' giving, represented in this month's sequence of the Four Letter Name, which moves from Hei (receiver) to Yud and Vav (givers) respectively, has the power to realign our relationship to the Divine and stimulate blessings to flow to us again, according to the proper natural order, from Above to below.

When we do not think that we are owed anything, and when we realize that we do not truly own anything or anyone, we can escape the gravitational field of possessiveness. When we praise Hashem, we, who are naturally 'receivers', are giving to the 'Giver'. This 'anti-gravity' giving can stimulate blessings to flow to us again, according to the proper natural order, from Above to below.

LETTER

There are twenty-two letters in the Aleph Beis. As the Torah, which is the 'Blueprint of Creation', is written in Hebrew, the *Lashon haKodesh* / Holy Tongue, the Sages teach that each of these twenty-two letters contain a host of metaphysical energies and creative potentials. According to the Sefer Yetzirah, a profound book of early Kabbalah that pays particular attention to the inner dimensions of the Hebrew letters, the twenty-two letters of the Aleph-Beis are divided into three categories: three "Mother Letters", seven "Double Letters" and twelve "Simple Letters". Each month is connected to one of the twelve Simple Letters.*

---

* For a more in-depth analysis of all three categories of Hebrew letters and their relationship to the calendar, please see the introductory volume in this series: *The Spiral of Time: Unraveling the Yearly Cycle*.

The letter associated with the month of Teves is Ayin (ע). The meaning of the word *Ayin* is 'eye', the seat of our optical potential. Related to this, there has been a long-standing debate between the *Chokrim* / philosophers and the *Mekubalim* / mystics as to which is the most important sense, hearing or sight? Certainly, all agree that from among the five senses, hearing and sight are the most 'important' or definitive for human consciousness. But the question remains as to which of these two is 'higher'.

Rabbi Avraham Ibn Ezra (Spain, 1089–1167) in his commentary [*Shemos*, 3:6, 20:1], along with Rabbi Levi ben Gershon (the Ralbag, France, 1288–1344) and many others, argue for the supremacy of 'sight' and insist that sight is the most refined sense [Note: *Reishis Chochmah*, Sha'ar haYirah 8. The Maharal, *Derech haChayim*, 2:9. *Sefer haBris*, 1, Ma'amar 17:5.]

On the other hand, Rabbi Mosheh ben Nachman [the Ramban, Spain/Israel, 1194 - c.1270, *Emunah uBitachon*, 18], along with his in-law Rabbeinu Yonah of Gerona [1200-1263, *Sha'arei Teshuvah*, Sha'ar 2:12], Rabbeinu Bachya ben Asher [Spain, 1340-1255, *Kad Kemach*, Zenus ha-Lev v'haAyin, 7], and later the Spanish Tzadik, Rabbi Yoseph Yavetz [in his commentary on *Avos* 6:2], argue that 'hearing' is the highest or deepest sense.

What is interesting to look at more closely, in the context of this debate, are the personalities of the individual rabbis involved. On the one hand, both the Ibn Ezra and the Ralbag, who argued for the supremacy of sight, were known philosophers; on the other hand, the others, who argued for the supremacy of sound, were either mystics or opponents of philosophy. The Ramban was a known Mekubal, as was Rabbeinu Bachya. Rabbeinu Yonah was a known opponent to the study of philosophy, and in fact was originally one of the foremost opponents to the philosophical treatise, *The Guide to the Perplexed*. Rabbi Yoseph Yavetz wrote an entire text arguing against the study of philosophy, entitled *Ohr haChayim*.

The philosophers argue that "Seeing is believing." In other words, what you see with the naked eye is what is real; the eye perceives the physical, therefore the physical is the most real and important dimension of Creation. The mystics contest this approach and insist that hearing is the most essential sense because the ear perceives what is beyond the physical and immediate reality. [Note, *Derech Pikudecha* (Dinov), Mitzvah 13.]

Rabbi Avraham, the son of the Rambam, a profound mystic and spiritual teacher (Egypt, 1186-1237), writes, "Although the sense of sight is the most refined according to the opinion of the philosophers, still, the pleasure that the soul receives from hearing and the awakening it arouses because of this is undeniable and clear. This sense [i.e., hearing] serves the soul (spirit of man) itself, and is very beneficial. It is especially required for the learning of wisdom and faith. It would be enough to remember that hearing is one of the great awakeners for the service of the heart" [*HaMaspik leOvdei Hashem*, 12].

Essentially, as mentioned, seeing is connected with physicality. What is present within one's immediate vicinity is what can be observed with the naked eye. This has led numerous Sages to directly equate the sense of sight with physical desires, lust and passionate possessiveness. *Ayin Roeh v'haLev Chomed* / "the eye sees and the heart desires" [*Rashi*, Bamidbar 15:39]. "A man only desires what his eyes first see" [*Sotah*, 8a. See also *Tosefos*, "Gemiri"]. While these teachings refer primarily to physical temptation, it is also true in general; we see something before our desire for it is aroused. The letter Ayin is therefore connected with the body and the desire to possess physical objects or people. This gives rise to the urge for instant gratification, the quality of Eisav, characterized by the desire to have whatever is in front of one at that very moment. Such is the overarching quality of possessiveness present in this month.

Ayin represents the number 70. What is the significance of this number? In the Torah, 70 is the full headcount of Yaakov's family when they descended into Egypt during the famine in Israel. Tradition teaches that there are 70 archetypal nations of the world. Additionally, there are six spatial dimensions — four lateral directions, plus up and down — and the central point is considered a 'seventh dimension'. Similarly, the physical world was created in six days, plus the Shabbos as the Divine seventh. 70 is an amplification of the power of seven multiplied by the 10 Sefiros, the channels of creation, which circulate and filter the Infinite Light of Hashem into finite manifestation. Therefore, the world or 'worldliness' is hinted at by the number 70.

Within the 70 root nations of the world, the letter Ayin is specifically connected with the nation of Edom, which is understood to be the root nation of the Roman Empire, and by extension, the essence of the contemporary Western World. The first word in the Torah to start with the letter Ayin is the word *Al* in the words *veChoshech **al** P'nei Tehom* / "and darkness was **upon** the surface of the deep" [*Bereishis*, 1:2]. There is great significance to the first time a word begins with a particular letter in the Torah.* According to

---

* *Bnei Yisaschar*, Iyyar, Ma'amar 3. A similar teaching is brought down in the name of the Vilna Gaon. *Toldos Yitzchak* (Talmid of Rav Isaac Chaver), p. 39b.

many Sages, the first time a particular letter appears as the beginning of a word, including its overall context, represents an expression of the letter's most primal energies.

Ayin is thus connected to the *P'nei Tehom* / surface of the deep, upon which it lies. It is interesting to note that Ayin, which as we mentioned means "eye", is specifically said to remain on the surface, as it were, of much deeper depths, which it cannot or will not penetrate. According to our sages [*Medrash Rabbah*, Bereishis, 2:4], *Choshech* / darkness alludes to the Greeks, whereas *Tehom* / the deep, alludes to Edom / Rome. Hence, Ayin, which represents the physical, and all the nations of the world, is intricately bound with Rome and the archetype of Edom.

Edom literally means 'red'. Indeed, in the world's imagination, the color most associated with the Roman Empire is red. This is based on the fact that Mars, the Roman deity of war and the patron of soldiers, was associated with the red planet, and thus the Roman soldiers, and even generals wore red, even though purple was considered a higher class of color. The nation and culture of Edom / Rome is rooted in the Torah archetype of Eisav, the brother of Yaakov. Indeed, Eisav is also called "the Red One" [*Bereishis*, 25:25].

The name *Eisav* begins with a letter Ayin. In fact, according to the Medrash *Osyos of Rabbi Akiva*, the letter Ayin symbolizes Eisav. Whereas Yaakov represents the soul, Eisav represents the body. The Torah describes Eisav's eating, drinking, walking and wanting.

For instance, the Gemara [*Baba Kama*, 55a] says that if someone sees the letter Tes in his dream it is a good sign, as Tes stands for *Tov* / good. Although there are other words in the Torah that begin with the letter Tes, still it is a good sign because the first time Tes appears is with the word *Tov* [*Bereishis*, 1:4].

He is present only in the immediate moment, trapped in the tangible now. In the Torah narrative, he always comes across as very physically potent, and yet overwhelmingly impulsive and almost entirely self-oriented. Rome is therefore characterized by the Sages as an intensely physical and materialistic nation.

As we have mentioned previously, there is a well-known episode in the Torah in which Eisav returns home, exhausted from vigorous hunting, and Yaakov is there cooking a stew. Upon entering, Eisav cries out, "Quick, let me have some of that red stew! I'm famished!"[*Bereishis*, 25:30]. Eisav first identifies the stew as 'red' — a visual, physical attribute, and then he desires to consume it. One of the *Tikkunim* / rectifications and realignments we might strive to perform in Teves is to avoid looking at things that increase our self-centered desires, our inner energies of Eisav and Tohu. This might be thought of as a kind of *Shemiras haAyin* / guarding of the eyes. Alternatively, a deeper level of the practice would be to not merely avert one's eyes from temptations, but to deepen one's vision, so to speak. By looking deeper, beneath the 'surface of the deep', one may connect to the spiritual meaning or potential of each person or thing that they encounter. Either way, this practice is particularly important when we are tired and looking for comfort, as was Eisav in this episode.

Teves begins with the last few days of Chanukah, upon which we light the flames of the Menorah, and are commanded specifically to "look at them." As we recite in the prayer following the lighting of the candles, "...These lights are holy; permission is not granted to utilize them, but only to look at them." As permission is only given to "look at them" (i.e., not to use them to look at or for other things), the custom is to gaze at them.

The flames of the Menorah are the visual antidote to chaotic, Tohu-based vision — seeing only the 'immediate' opportunities or implications while overlooking the bigger picture and deeper perspective. The Chanukah lights have the power to heal our eyes, and to rectify and undo the damage of any negative sight. [See *Sifsei Tzadikim*, Chanukah 1. *Avodas Yisrael. Beis Avraham*, Chanukah, 4. *Imrei Noam*, 50.]

More than simply a magical, mystical healing of our sight, the act of gazing at the delicate, dancing flames naturally heals a person from only seeing the surface appearance of things. The nature of a flame is to to constantly change. There is thus no fixed image in a flame. The moment you try to freeze the fire with your eyes in order to define it, the image disappears. Furthermore, a flame leaps upward, drawing and directing one's attention to what is Above. Both of these dynamics help us to see the world, others and ourselves in a more selfless, holy, dynamic and transcendent way. This is the perfect antidote for *Tohu* seeing, which is prone to fixating on static images and desiring to immediately possess and own them. This type of seeing alienates one from others, as it tends towards static objectification of dynamic subjects, as well as cuts one from a deeper sense of any future or higher purpose. Realizing instead the impermanence of all images, while letting them direct us to the reality Above, removes from us the chaotic impatience of Eisav and strengthens in us the equanimity and higher vision of Yaakov.

☾

NAME OF THE MONTH

*A*CCORDING TO THE TORAH, NAMES ARE VERY POWERFUL [*Yumah*, 83b. *Tanchuma*, Hazinu. *Berachos*, 7b]. Comprised as they are of Hebrew letters, they represent and define the energy or attributes of that which is named [*Tanya*, Sha'ar HaYichud Veha'emunah, 1]. Our names, for instance, unlock and reveal hidden potentials present within our own spiritual makeup. Similarly, names of other people, places, and periods of time provide subtle hints as to their deeper purpose or poetic significance. Additionally, changing one's name is akin to a kind of rebirth; some might even say that a change of name initiates a change of *Mazal* [*Rashi*, Bereishis 15:5. *Rosh Hashanah*, 16b. Yerushalmi, *Shabbos*, 6:39. *Ramah*, Yoreh Deah, 335:10].

Each of the twelve months of the year has a distinct name, and every name has a meaning. According to our Sages, the current names we have for the months were imported to our tradition upon our return to Israel from the Babylonian Exile. [They can in fact be traced to ancient Babylonian or Akkadian names. See *Yerushalmi*, Rosh Hashanah, 1:2. *Medrash Rabbah*, Bereishis, 48:9.] In the times before the Babylonian Exile, the names of the months were mostly known by their number in the sequence of the year. For example, the month of Av was called the Fifth Month, and Cheshvan was known as the Eighth Month.

The Akkadian/Babylonian word *Teves*, when translated into Hebrew, is related to the word *Tov* / goodness. It can also be broken down into two words: *Tov Bas*. [See Maharam miPanu, *Asara Ma'amaros*, Ma'amar Chikur Din, 3:4.] In Talmudic language, *Bas* may be used to refer to matters of physical intimacy, and thus in such a case *Tov Bas* literally means 'good for intimacy' [*Ben Yehoyada*, Megilah, 13a]. Teves is therefore a 'good' month in which to create a Tikkun for issues relating to physical intimacy.

Physical intimacy can be the holiest and purest action in the world, as the Ramban writes [*Iggeres HaKodesh*. *Ramban*, Shemos, 30:13. See however *Moreh Nevuchim*, 3:8.]. It can embody genuine unity, the greatest quality of 'goodness' in the world. When approached with sensitivity and sanctity, it can be a taste or preview of the ultimate Unity of the World to Come. [On the other hand, see *Berachos*, 57b.]

Hashem's Presence, the essence and root of all *Yichud* / oneness, rests upon a couple who honor the holiness of intimacy, not to mention each other [*Sotah*, 17a]. In the words of the Zohar, "The Divine Presence rests upon the marital space when spouses are united in love and holiness." The *Ko'ach Ein Sof* / power of Infinity is revealed within Yichud, and that power is the power to be like the Creator, as a new child is thereby created.

Intimacy is potentially the holiest human encounter, yet, because it is so deep and holy, when performed without intention, or worse, without respect for the dynamic subjectivity of the other, it can perpetuate the worst evils and imbalances in the universe.

Teves is spelled Tes-Beis-Tav. As mentioned, we learn the primal significance of a letter by the first time a word begins with that letter in the Torah. The first words in the Torah to begin with these three letters are:

Tes — *Tov* / good
Beis — *Bereishis*, / 'in the beginning' or 'in the head'
Tav — *Tohu* / chaos.

Therefore, one meaning of *Teves* is, 'There is good within the head or source of Tohu.'

The World of Tohu is the source of all physical reality including the animals, our physical body, and the animal self within including its attendant ego and energy of brute force. In contrast, all spiritual reality including our souls and psycho-spiritual dimensions are rooted in the World of Tikkun. The physical body has immediate needs. When it is hungry it will eat anything, even foods that can be harmful. Without the mind, the body is chaotic. A starving person who eats too quickly can die, and many have done so because of this chaotic impulse of the body.

The World of Tohu preceded, or precedes, the world as we know it. It is therefore a very primal and primordial reality. Although it is characterized by chaos and unpredictability, it is an exceptionally exalted reality, since it is 'chronologically' closer to the Source of Emanation. In terms of the ultimate 'objective', the purpose and intention of Creation, the world of Tikkun is supreme. Yet in terms of the 'process' or power of Creation, Tohu is higher as it emerges first. The World of Tikkun appears only after the vessels of the world of Tohu have been broken. It is therefore the sparks of the primordial Light of Tohu that are scattered throughout our reality, which require our gathering and elevation within the new vessels of Tikkun.

The 'head' or *source* of Tohu is the highest of the high. It is beyond the impulsive and chaotic physical expressions of Tohu in this world, and it is also beyond the soulful orderliness of Tikkun. In the head or root of Tohu there is the potential for tremendous goodness, even higher than the goodness or holiness of the soul, as it were.

The numeric value of the word *Teves* is 411 (Tes/9 + Beis/2 + Tav/400 = 411), as is the word *Tohu* (Tav/400 + Hei/5 + Vav/6 = 411).

Eisav represents Tohu, while Yaakov, his twin brother, represents Tikkun. The 'head' (or Rosh, as in *be-Reishis*) of Eisav is holy and good (*Tov*): "The head of Eisav is buried by the feet of Yitzchak (or Yaakov)." [See *Targum Yonason, Bereishis*, 50:13. *Sotah*, 13a.] At Yaakov's funeral Eisav was struck and decapitated, and his head rolled into the cave where the Patriarchs and Matriarchs were buried, where

Yaakov was being buried. And so the 'head', the essence and root, of Eisav returned back to its holy source and was buried together with his parents and the other Patriarchs and Matriarchs in the holy Cave of Machpelah.

During Teves, we have the *Ko'ach* / strength to convert the impulsiveness of the physical body, and all unhealthy Tohu energy, into a positive force for the ultimate good. We have the ability to tap into *Tov beReishis Tohu* / the goodness within the Head of Tohu. *Teves* begins with the letter Tes. Tes stands for *Tov*, as the first time the letter Tes appears in the Torah at the beginning of a word is with the word Tov — good [*Baba Kamah*, 55a]. We can begin to facilitate this process by harnessing the power of the good eye, the *Ayin Tov*. On the other hand, the chaos of physicality and selfish desire causes an *Ayin haRa* / evil eye to project and spread jealousy and negativity. The way to nullify and transform an Ayin haRa when it is hurled at you is to see everything and everyone, including yourself, with an *Ayin Tov* / good eye.

We activate and strengthen our Ayin Tov by gazing at the lights of the Menorah in the beginning of the month. Through this powerful healing of our eyes, not only do we rectify and undo the damage of all negative sight and vision, we empower ourselves to see and interact with the world through a lens of selfless goodness, holiness, humility and transcendence.

The letter of the month, Ayin, also means 'eye'. When speaking about the Ayin Tov, we are specifically referring to the right eye, which is the 'side of Chesed', alluding to loving-kindness. When we view others with Chesed, with an Ayin Tov, we can rectify or enhance the goodness in our relationships, which is our task in Teves, the month connected with intimacy.

Teves is one of the only fully harsh months of the year, and, as the Zohar explains it is therefore intimately connected with Eisav.*

Another meaning of the syllables of the word *Teves* — *Tov Bas* — is 'stopping the good'. [Maharam miPanu, *Assarah Ma'amaros*, Ma'amar Chikur Din, 3:4. Teves is called 'bad days', *Zohar* 3, p. 259a.] Yet, through our inner work of elevated intention and attention, we can convert the chaotic impulsiveness of the physical body and the unhealthy energy of Tohu into fuel for our soul. We can take this unbridled passionate energy, which is the cause of arrogance, ego and possessiveness, and direct it into the vessels of Tikkun. When these two worlds are brought together, the primal energy of Tohu and the purified vessels of Tikkun, then nothing can stand in the way of the ultimate redemption of reality in all its aspects.

---

*Nisan, Iyyar and Sivan belong to Yaakov. Tamuz, Av and Elul belong to Eisav. Yaakov was able to elevate half of Av and Elul. Tamuz, a time of unbearable heat, remains unredeemed, and is thus a time of harsh judgment. Additionally, Tishrei, Cheshvan and Kislev belong to Yaakov, whereas Teves, Shevat and Adar belong to Eisav. Similarly, Yaakov was able to elevate half of Shevat and the month of Adar, while Teves remained unredeemed. Thus, the coldest month of Teves and the hottest month of Tamuz are still entirely connected to Eisav. *Avodas Yisrael* (Koznitz) Vayigash. *Sheim meShemuel*, VaEira.

SENSE

The conventional world identifies five senses, yet *Sefer Yetzirah* speaks of twelve *Chushin* / senses. In addition to the more commonly understood definition of what comprises our 'senses', the word *chush* can also mean, 'a sensitive level of perception, understanding, appreciation and skill' in relation to a particular psycho-spiritual process or function. For example, a 'sense of sleep' is a deep understanding and appreciation of sleep which includes both: what sleep represents spiritually, as well as the practical skills and abilities that make one's experience of sleep both peaceful and beneficial.

These twelve *Chushim* are also the twelve activities that the Torah describes the Creator performing in the perpetual process of maintaining the world [*Pirush haRavad, Sefer Yetzirah*]. As we are created in the Divine image we also possess all twelve *Chushim*, at least in potential.* Every month gives us the ability and strength to expand our vessels (potentials) for a particular *Chush*, along with its corresponding Divine Attributes. When we align and refine our consciousness via these *Chushim*, we can harness the qualities of each month in a most profound and meaningful way.

According to the Arizal, the *Chush* / sense of Teves is *Rogez* / wrath and anger. Anger harms the body, especially the eyes: "My eyes have grown dim because of anger (or sorrow)." [*Iyov*, 17:7. See also *Tehillim*, 6:8 and 31:10.] Anger clouds our higher vision and obscures our deeper in-sight.

There is however also a concept of *Rogez d'Kedushah* / holy and noble anger [*Berachos*, 5a], as in *Pachad Yitzchak* / terror of Yitzchak, also known as *Rugza d'Rabbanan* / anger of the Sages, and *Rischa d'Oraysa* / the fire of the Torah [*Ta'anis*, 4a]. "Torah is fire, and the Torah fires them up" [*Zohar* 2, p, 182b]. In the language of the holy Zohar, "There are two types of wrath. One type of wrath is blessed from Above and from below and is called 'blessed'.... There is also a type of wrath which is cursed Above and below, and we have learned that it is called 'cursed'"[*Zohar* 1, p, 184a]. It should be made clear, though, that the distinction between destructive, ego-based

---

* Even if one is blind, for example, he always has the *potential* for sight — it's just that he is currently missing the physical vessels (capacity) for it [*Pirush HaGra, Hakdamah, Sefer Yetzirah*]. However, the sense of sight is included in the person's Divine image, as it were. Obviously, a physically blind person could have immense vessels for spiritual sight.

anger and productive, egoless anger can be very subtle and hardly distinguishable [*Mei haShiloach* 2. p, 102]. Unfortunately, unholy and ego-driven anger is by far the more common, this is the 'anger of Eisav'. This anger is impulsive, chaotic, explosive and hurtful. Unholy anger is connected with 'blood', which is the sign of Eisav. Significantly, as will shortly be explored, the body part of this month is the *Kaved* / liver which is full of blood and an organ related to anger. Eisav, appropriately, is also associated with the liver [*Tikkunei Zohar*, Tikkun 21].

Unholy anger is generally referred to as *Ka'as*. *Ka'as* is spelled Kuf-Ayin-Samach. The middle letter is Ayin (which, again, also means 'eye'), symbolizing the 'inner' (or middle) eye. The word *Kas* (Kuf-Samach, without the Ayin) is the root word for 'hidden'. In unholy anger, our inner eye is hidden, and all we can see is our angry, self-oriented, egoic perception of reality.

The Sensation vs. the Narrative:

To go a little deeper into the concept of anger, we must first understand how it is a neutral sense, like the 'sense' of eating or taste.*First, a distinction has to be made between the 'narrative' that gives rise to anger, and the sensation or visceral reaction in the body when experiencing anger. The narrative and the interpretation of anger is what is negative, destructive and useless, whereas the sensation of the anger itself is, for the most part, neutral, and may even be channeled for positive ends.

An even deeper layer of the Chush of Rogez is the positive po-

---
* The Chush of eating and taste was explored in the book on the Month of Shevat.

tential of anger. This layer is revealed when the 'sensations of anger' are not attached to any negative narrative. In such a case, when one is able to strip the sensations of anger from their perceived source in a negative story, one is simply left with a rush of neuro-chemical reactions and powerful sensations streaming through the body. The negative effects of Rogez only manifest when we allow the narrative of anger to guide our actions, often resulting in reactive attempts to stop the discomfort of the sensations or to protect ourselves from being further hurt. This negative, chaotic response can even lead to acts of violence, Heaven forbid.

The pure sensation of anger is very different than its attendant narrative, which we so often mistake for its source. For instance, if someone does something to you that your ego considers a violation or injury, the mind will offer a narrative to justify your emotional and physical responses. For example, say you are a writer and someone tells you that your books are horrible, you may become angry. In this instance, there are two things happening: a) there is a strong physical experience: sensations in the body, a racing or palpitating heart, sweating, etc., and b) these sensations are then interpreted as a need to retaliate; the mental and emotional anger seething in your soul is thus directed toward the 'offender' in your narrative. It is important to note that although the sensations in the body were originally triggered by a narrative, yet, if that narrative is interrupted or removed, the sensations still remain. However, without the justification of the story, they are just that — mere sensations. They do not necessarily cause one to act or lash out further in an attempt to avenge one's perceived insult. In fact, they may even be witnessed or contemplated until they eventually dissipate, as all sensations, when left to themselves, always do.

Since, as we have established, sensations in themselves are basically neutral energies, they can be used for positive action instead of retribution, if properly channeled. By untangling yourself from your angry or victim narrative, you will be able to objectively observe the intense sensations rising up and receding again. When you have attained such objectivity, you can manage the sensations, rather than them managing you, and you can then employ the aroused energies for positive and productive action, rather than the opposite. When you are free of your often unconsciously constructed narrative, your natural sensations are no longer 'your' anger or 'your' hurt, rather they are just a flow of physiological mobilization, like a strong wind. This wind can fill the sail of proper conduct, such as a good deed done with zest, it can fuel a run around the block that brings the body and mind back into balance, or it can drive one into a self-destructive frenzy — ultimately, it is up to you what to do with your anger and energy.

The actual sensations of anger are overwhelming and raw, much like the brute force of Eisav. These sensations alert the body, and suggest that it act immediately, like a hunter in the fields who spots his prey. They activate a sharpness and heightened sensitivity to our surroundings and to life in general. This state can obviously be very beneficial, and in fact has played a decisive role in our species' survival over the ages. However, if you live your life on autopilot and your sensations are unconsciously entangled with your personal narratives, then instinctively you will act out with chaos and force, rather than strategy and sensitivity. When someone insults you or your work, you will immediately insult them back, or even raise your hand to strike them, Heaven forbid. However, if you can separate your sensations from your story, and just be present in the neutral space of pure, raw sensation and embodied experience, you can just feel their inevitable ebb and flow. Alternatively, you can even make a conscious decision to yoke and ride the original sensations, letting them increase your zest and focus and skillful action. You can thus channel the Chush of Rogez into a creative breakthrough.

However, as soon as you subscribe to and succumb to the narrative of your anger, the anger becomes your master and you lose your clarity and ability to freely navigate a path through your experience. Your responses then become entirely reactive, egoic, and fear-based. Inevitably, if you are not the master over your anger then your anger is a master over you. When you are mastered by your anger you lose your *Da'as* / consciousness, and capacity to see clearly and choose wisely. In the stark words of our Sages, "One who is angry, if he is wise, his wisdom will leave him; if he is prophetic, he will lose his prophecy" [*Pesachim*, 66b].

A wise person is someone who can 'see the future' [*Tamid*, 32a], almost like a prophet. But what does this mean? Most people only see what is right in front of them, they only perceive the immediate implications of their actions in the moment. In contrast, a wise person is able to see that which is beyond their current reality; in other words, they can see the future consequences of their present actions [*Avos*, 2:9]. Their vision therefore penetrates beyond the immediate and beneath the surface of a given situation. Yet one who gets angry gets stuck in the narrowness of the immediate moment, and loses his awareness of a potential future. He 'sees red', and thereby loses his wisdom and squanders the prophet-like vision of his inner eye.

Even when we encounter social or moral injustices which rightly stimulate our anger, if we unconsciously attach ourselves to the narrative driving our emotions, the anger becomes our master and our chaotic reactivity produces ineffective or even detrimental responses. When we are controlled by anger, our responses are based in the weakness of egoic fear, rather than in the strength of selfless Da'as. With Da'as we can express ourselves calmly and consciously, with "the voice of Yaakov", even while we may still feel in our body the sensation of being a hunter on high alert, characterized by "the hands of Eisav". Thus, we can channel the *Ohr* / light of Tohu into and through the *Kelim* / vessels of Tikkun. Without attaching ourselves to the self-centered narratives of our life, we can truly connect with others. In Teves we must work on connecting to others in the deepest way.

Stripping the Sensation from the Narrative:

In order to do this we need to first learn how to strip the sensation from the narrative. But how? If the sensations are created by the narrative in the first place, and then they become completely entangled with the narrative, how can we mentally undo their bond?

In every experience in life there are two elements: the experience or feeling, and the experiencer or feeler. Whenever you are experiencing a feeling, there is a 'you' that is experiencing it. But 'you' are not the experience itself. In other words, when you experience anger, you are not the anger. In other words: 'you' are not angry, 'you' are experiencing the sensations of anger. To disentangle yourself, start by noticing this existential separation between yourself and your experience.

The experiencer, the I, is spacious, fluid, and full of life, whereas the actual experience, when defined and enclosed by a narrative, is rigid, statice, and dead.

When anger is triggered because of your attachment to a particular narrative of violation, pause for a moment. Without dropping the sensation of anger or the swelling of energy, allow yourself just to feel and observe without reacting in any way.

If a person would attain a state of never feeling anger at all, it would be a non-human state, and therefore not desirable. Stoicism or indifference is cold and lifeless. By allowing ourselves to fully feel the sensations of anger, we ensure that we do not become indifferent and non-human, rather, we become more alive, engaged and responsive to life. By letting go of our narratives and staying with sensations, we allow ourselves to be present in such a way that emotions do not rule us and limit our responses. Then our activism, our relating to others, our creative and spiritual practices, can all become truly successful and influential in the most positive and productive ways. As a result, we will be closer to effectively stopping the injustice or injury that originally stimulated our anger in the first place, rather than remaining stuck in an endless wheel of suffering.

This is the deeper meaning of the positivity of the Chush of Rogez. It is not about the narrative of anger or the acts that arise out of anger, but rather we are referring to the power of the raw 'sensation' that we may describe as anger. How we use this sensation makes all the difference and determines whether our anger is ultimately negative and destructive or positive and productive.

When we Subscribe to the Narrative:

The Zohar says that when we are angry, when we sacrifice our free-will to the narrative of anger, we are like an idol worshipper. [See *Zohar* 1, Bereishis, 27:2. *Zohar* 3, Korach 179:1.] "Whoever becomes angry is like an idol worshipper"* [Rambam, *Hilchos De'os*, Chap. 2:33].

Whenever we are stuck and hold onto a fixed image of self or fasten our imagination on what we think is to be expected and the results do not match up to our expectations, we become angry. This is the underlying narrative of anger, which is often tied up with our expectations. Our anger is inflamed when our ego, or our internal picture of how our life should be and evolve, is disrupted. We construct in our minds certain static or stagnant images of who we are, how the events in our life should look, and, based on this, how people should act in relation to us. When life, which is not at all static, veers off course, we experience sensations of upset or anger.

---

* While there is no explicit source for this teaching found in the Gemara or even in other Medrashic sources (besides the Zohar), the Gemara does equate anger with the sin of idol worship: "If someone tears garments in anger he is like an idol worshipper" [*Shabbos*, 105b]. Yet, there is an apparent distinction between someone simply being angry versus someone acting on his anger. *Maharatz Chayus*, ad loc.: "Whoever gets angry, various forms of Gehenom take hold" [*Nedarim*, 22a]. It seems that an earlier version of this statement was as follows: "One who angers is as if he served idols" [*Teshuvas haRashbash*, Siman 370].

Then we may get swept up in thoughts: how could so-and-so say or do that to me? Or how could this be happening to *me*? All these are statements of an ego in distress, a perception of life gone askew.

The egoic perception of reality, thinking we know how life ought to be and how events are meant to unfold, is the source of anger. If you are driving carefully down the highway and a car comes out of nowhere and cuts you off, you might become agitated: 'This is not supposed to happen to a careful driver like me!' Things did not work out the way you thought they should or assumed they would, according to your fixed narrative and fixed identity. As such, ego is the root of anger; our fragile ego lives in perpetual fear of being disturbed or violated.

Our ego sets up a conscious or subconscious outline that our life should fulfill, but life never follows a preconceived program. When we believe that our ego has been tampered with, if we do not possess a measure of self-mastery, we will lash out in anger against the other, or perhaps even against all others. We foolishly believe this outwardly-directed anger will help us. When our feeling of pride has been tarnished, we somehow believe that displaying anger against the other will boost, secure or safeguard us. But the ego we are defending is not what or who we really are. Tragically, many people unconsciously blame others for their own shortcomings; they use their anger as a weapon to defend their egoic stories of competency or correctness. Thus they exile themselves more and more from their true competency and connection to their souls.

People who see themselves as the center of the universe to the exclusion of all others are *self-idolaters*, separating themselves from the entire web of life. This is certainly an extreme case. However, underlying even the more common emotion of anger there is also a subtle sense of heresy [*Tanya*, Iggeres HaKodesh, 25]. By chaotically reacting in anger we are saying that we reject the Creator's Light which has become manifest to us in the car that cut us off, or the person who insulted us. [Even though this person has free choice, in relation to us, it is the Creator's Light itself that is appearing as the car cutting us off or the insulting comment.] Our anger is, in a sense, arrogantly asserting that our idea of how things should unfold in life is better than Hashem's.

In submitting to the negative aspects of anger, a person is overtly denying or rejecting *Hashgacha P'ratis* / Divine Providence. By rejecting a certain manifestation of Hashem, one is attempting to claim their own providence and rulership over life. The attempt to reject the One means that 'I believe I am separate and sovereign'. If I am rejecting what is being revealed to me, I am exacerbating the sense of a separate 'me'.

This is the reason why our sages say, "Whoever becomes angry is like an idol-worshipper." When one loses himself in anger, he is declaring himself a deity and demanding that others venerate him. By impulsively asserting, 'I know better, I think it should be this way,' and ultimately, 'Hashem has it wrong,' G-d forbid — he is irrationally rejecting the Source of Wisdom and setting himself up as the true source of wisdom.

The fast day of the Tenth of Teves, the one day that stands out and characterizes Teves which we will explore in more depth shortly, teaches us the consequences of idol-worship. On this day the

Babylonian siege of *Yerushalayim* / Jerusalem began [*Yechezkel*, 24:2. *Rosh Hashanah*, 18b]. The cause of the Babylonian Exile, the first exile from Jerusalem, was said to be the idol worship of the people of Israel at that time [*Yumah*, 9b]. This siege, initiated by our psycho-spiritual shortcomings, ended in a tragic exile from the physical manifestation of our spiritual and communal center.

According to the Gaonim, Teves is connected to the 'sense' of *Sechok* / laughter. Laughter is another intense sensation — like the sensation of anger — that can grip the body. However, in contrast to anger, laughter usually passes through our system and dissipates without getting stuck. With regards to anger, if we can let go of the associated narrative and hold onto a consciousness of Divinity, we can convert the self-destructive 'anger of Eisav' to holy and productive anger, utilizing the visceral and emotional sensations for positive actions. The same is true with the sensation of laughter. There is holy laughter and unholy laughter, a laughter of release and a laughter of cynicism, as will be explored in the volume on Adar. Suffice it to say, we always have the ability to use a given sensation for the positive.

♈

SIGN

*E*ACH MONTH CONTAINS THE ZODIAC INFLUENCE OF A PARTICULAR constellation, called the *Mazal*. A constellation is comprised of a perceivably patterned grouping of visible stars. Today, we count 88 constellations in the night sky. Out of all of these, one constellation is predominantly visible on the horizon at the beginning of each month.

Indeed, each constellation refracts the light of the cosmos differently, alternately reflecting times that are more conducive to war, and times that are more conducive for peace to flourish, for example [*Yalkut Reuveini, Bereishis,* Oys 56]. The *Zohar* teaches that each sign can manifest positively or negatively [*Zohar* 3, 282a]. In other words, the constellations can have either a productive or a destructive influence in one's life. It is important to keep in mind, however, that even if our proclivities are innate or celestially influenced, we still possess the free choice of response to the situations that arise in our life. In other words, we have the ability to choose how to reflect back what has been projected onto us, even from the stars. For example, a person born under the influence of Mars may have a tendency to be involved with blood, but he or she also has the ability to employ this inherent tendency for good or ill; such a person could therefore choose to be a violent criminal or a life-saving surgeon [*Shabbos*, 156a].

Due to the prevailing popular belief that the stars exert a kind of fatalistic influence upon world history and human development, we need to repeatedly emphasize that anyone can rise above these influences altogether and be unaffected by them. Despite all the forces and influences in our life — physical and psychological conditions, upbringing, education, environment, financial status, etc. — we always have the freedom to choose. We have the choice to live as either the *effect* of our conditions (as passive receivers of what life serves us), or as the *cause* of what comes next, thereby becoming proactive co-creators of our lives. When we begin to live more proactively, the influences of our birth constellation and the *Mazal* of each month function less as positive or negative *influences*, and more as *tools* that can help us climb ever higher into our freedom of being.

The constellation of Teves is a *Gedi* / goat, corresponding to Capricorn. The numerical value of the word Gedi is 17, the same value as *Tov* / good; additionally, the Hebrew word *Gedi* (גדי) contains the letters גד (*Gad*), which suggests 'good luck'. [See *Rashi* on Bereishis, 30:11, quoting *Medrash Rabbah*, 71:9. See also *Targum Yonason Ben Uziel*.] Despite its inherent challenges, the month of Teves is ultimately *Tov*; as mentioned previously, the word Teves is intimately related to the word *Tov*.

A wild goat represents our animal or physical nature, as well as a potential force of negativity. Our sages tell us that once, a student, seeing that his teacher was open and in an expansive mood, asked him, "Why are goats first in the pack and then sheep?" The teacher answered, "This is similar to the workings of the world… First comes darkness, then light" [*Shabbos*, 77b]. Rashi explains: goats are generally black and sheep white. Goats therefore represent 'night', darkness, and a destructive force. White, gentle sheep represent 'daytime', light, and positivity. One way we actually observe this 'negativity' in goats [of course animals do not have free choice and stand beyond any moral judgment], is the way they graze excessively, sometimes eroding and destroying the pasturing land, unlike the more well-mannered sheep.

Another word for goat, *Se'ir*, can also mean 'to storm' or 'hairy'. *Se'ir* is a reference to Eisav who is called *Ish Seir* / a hairy person [*Medrash Rabbah*, Bereishis, 65:15]. Indeed, the words *Se'ir* / goat and *Sa'ir* / hair are spelled with the same letters, and the *Se'ir* / goat also alludes to a person who is hairy like a goat [*Akeidas Yitzchak*, Parshas Ach'rei Mos, Sha'ar 63].

Rabbi Yehudah Loew of Prague, known as the Maharal (1512-1609), points out [*Chidushei Agados*, Shabbos] that the word *Se'ir* is numerically 580, the same as *haYetzer haRa* / the negative inclination. *Yetzer haRa* is more accurately translated as 'the ego-based, animal instincts or tendencies'. This is our inclination that prompts us to seek out gratification in the moment, in the now [*Akeidas Yitzchak*, Parshas Naso, Sha'ar 73]. This goat-like, wild, stormy energy is the embodiment of the Tohu quality of Eisav, and his drive for immediate gratification. However, this inclination also has positive future-oriented aspects as well, if channeled appropriately. According to the Sages: "...Were it not for our Yetzer nothing would compel us to build a home, enter a relationship, have children, or do business" [*Medrash Rabbah*, Bereishis, 9:7].

Yaakov tells his mother Rivkah, "...My brother Eisav is a hairy man (*Ish Sa'ir*) and I am smooth-skinned" [*Bereishis*, 27:11]. In order to make his father Yitzhak believe that he was Eisav, Yaakov put a hairy goat hide on his hands. He did this because he wanted his father's blessings for physical wealth and pleasure, and, as a result, Yitzchak proceeded to bless him with "...the dew of the Heavens and the fats of the Land...." These are the blessings of the body which Yitzchak first intended for Eisav, the 'man of the fields'. Only when Yaakov donned the hairy goat hides of Eisav was he able to trick his father into giving him these blessings.

Later on in the narrative, many year after receiving these blessings, Yaakov has become wealthy. He crosses a river to retrieve some belongings he accidentally left behind and finds himself alone. There he wrestles with the *Sar*, the guiding angel, of Eisav, the entire night. "And Yaakov was left alone, and a man (the prince/angel of Eisav) wrestled with him until the break of dawn. When he saw that he could not prevail against him, he touched the socket of his hip.... And he (the angel) said, 'Let me go, for dawn is breaking,' but he (Yaakov) said, 'I will not let you go unless you have blessed me'" [*Bereishis*, 32:25- 27]. After struggling all night, the angel is ready to leave, and Yaakov first asks the angel to bless him. Why would he ask for a blessing from a character (whether subjective or objective) with whom he has just been fighting?

Besides being actual people, Eisav and Yaakov are also archetypes. Eisav represents the physical body and the material world, while Yaakov represents the soul and the spiritual world. Yaakov therefore wrestles with the angel of Eisav in order to include the physical within the spiritual. He did not want to merely transcend the physical. This is why Yaakov asked the angel of Eisav for a 'blessing' — a blessing of the material world. And this is the key to one of the main Tikkunim or elevations that can occur in Teves, focused as it is on refining our relationship to physical intimacy and relationships. Indeed, this struggle is mystically connected with the months of Teves and Shevat [*Mishnas Chasidim*, Maseches Teves-Shevat, 2].

Capricorn is related to the element of earth. People born under the sign of Capricorn show a deep connection to the earthly and material realm, and often to family and home, making them good caretakers, nurturers and providers. On the other hand, when out of balance, Capricorns can be possessive and materialistic, like Eisav. For everyone, Teves is a good month to work on selfish materialism and our sense of ownership or entitlement. The best way to do this is to practice conscious giving. This giving must not be done in order to receive from the other, rather, the opposite: we must receive our material abundance in order to give. This energetic dynamic is reflected in the letter sequence of this month's permutation of Hashem's name, as discussed previously. Recall that the pattern of the letters, which represent the flow of *Shefa* / abundance, consistently moves from the Hei (receiver) to the Yud and then the Vav (givers), mirroring this process of 'receiving in order to give'. It should also be noted that the word *Kabbalah* actually means 'receiving'. But tradition teaches that it is not enough to just receive, a vessel must give over what it has received, or it will simply spill or shatter, as happened to the Sefiros in the world of Tohu, as discussed previously. The World of Tikkun itself is defined by this very approach of 'receiving in order to give'. When this has been accomplished, the negativity of the material realm will be neutralized, and physicality will be included within a more expansive spiritual context, unifying all of reality into one true blessing.

TRIBE

Every month of the year is connected with one of the Twelve Tribes of Israel, the sons of Yaakov / Jacob [*Sefer Yetzirah*; Medrash, *Osyos Rebbe Akiva*, Dalet].

The tribe associated with Teves is Dan. The meaning of the word *Dan* is 'strength' or 'judge' [*Bereishis*, 30:6]. Judgment depends on seeing, as in, "A judge only judges by what his eyes can see" [*Sanhedrin*, 6a]. As this month is connected with the letter Ayin (alluding to the eyes), and with the physical world, it is abundantly clear that we are discussing a type of judgment which is based in the empirical, physical world, implying specifically that which is seen with the physical eye.

The word *Dan* also suggests the concept of *Din* / harsh judgment or contractions of the flow of blessing. There are qualities of Din present in this month, but we can elevate them, and transform them through the power of Dan. In truth, Dan's strength is predicated on his ability to transform Din.

Our sages relate how Chushim, the deaf son of Dan, fought and decapitated Eisav, as explored previously [*Sotah,* 13a]. After Yaakov passed away in Egypt the sons of Yaakov, including Yoseph, brought his coffin to be buried in the *Me'aras haMachpelah* / the Cave of Machpelah. When they finally showed up at the burial site, Eisav was there waiting, claiming as his own the right to be buried there. Yoseph told him that there is a contract in Egypt showing that Yaakov purchased the Me'aras haMachpelah, and Naftali, 'the swift one', hurried back to Egypt to retrieve this contract. Meanwhile, Chushim wanted to know why they were not burying Yaakov, and he was told that Eisav was holding them back from doing so. Upon hearing this, he grabbed a sword and removed Eisav's head. His head rolled into the cave, next to where Avraham and Sarah, Yitzchak and Rivkah and Leah were all buried. His body, however, was returned to Edom to be buried there. In the context of Teves, this story represents the redemptive potential that resides within the "head of Tohu", as Tohu is connected to Eisav, as discussed. Accordingly, his body is discarded, but his head is reabsorbed back into the realm of *Kedusha* / holiness, alongside the other Patriarchs and Matriarchs.

Chushim, in this account, represents noble and holy 'anger', illuminating its redemptive potential. Thus his name, *Chushim* (without the Vav), is numerically 358, which is the same value (and actually the same letters) as the word *Moshiach*. The head of Eisav represents the highest expression of the brute energy of Tohu — the pure power of the World of Chaos. By removing Eisav's head, Chushim elevated this 'source of chaos' into the world of Tikkun. This is the meaning of the 'head', the source of Eisav, being buried (included) in the cave of Machpelah, a place of great holiness and Tikkun. As *Chushim* has the same four letters as the word *Moshiach*, he is able to tap into the very root power of Eisav, and bring it into the *Kelim* / 'vessels' of Tikkun, a process which will be completed with the coming of Moshiach.

In the month of Teves, we too have an additional *Koach* / power to elevate the chaos and raw energy that is at the root of our own brute physicality, and to place it within an exalted and meaningful context of transcendence.

Dan Yadin Amo / "Dan shall judge his people" [*Bereishis*, 49:16]. Rashi and the Ramban say this verse refers to Shimshon, the great and mighty warrior who was a member of the Tribe of Dan [*Sotah*, 10a]. The Rashbam, however, says the verse doesn't refer to a single individual, rather it is a prophecy about the entire tribe of Dan, as they were very great warriors. In the Desert this tribe traveled behind the other tribes in order to see oncoming physical threats and protect the entire nation.

Besides being just physical warriors, the Tribe of Dan traveled at the back of the formation in the Desert, so as to literally be a *meAseph* / gathering of what was dropped. On a deeper level, this means they had the ability to stand outside the physical and spiritual protection of the Clouds of Glory, and to bring back and gather all the stray holy sparks which had fallen furthest from their source into their proper fold. They were thus able to locate the 'head', the deepest spark, even within a person like Eisav, and 'gather' or integrate and incorporate it into the cave of holiness.

Eisav engraved the image of a snake on his thigh [*Sefer Tziyoni*, Toldos, p. 44. Shaloh haKodesh, *Torah She'b'Ksav*, Tzon Yoseph, 12], and Yaakov blessed Dan to be like a snake [*Bereishis*, 49:17]. Indeed, Dan's sapphire-colored flag had a snake drawn on it [*Medrash Rabbah*, Bamidbar 2:7]. This illustrates Dan's inner connection to Eisav, and his ability to gather, harness, transform and elevate the raw energy of Tohu.

In Teves, we too are given this ability and task, empowered by the tribe and energies of this month. We are also given the spiritual Koach to harness and channel the Din of Teves, and even 'anger' itself, in order to integrate everything, even seemingly negative energies, into the World of Tikkun. The Tribe of Dan teaches us that one way we can elevate our own brute physicality and 'chaos' is by using it to protect or rescue others from danger.

BODY PART

*E*ACH MONTH IS CONNECTED WITH THE GENERAL ENERGY and particular vibration of a specific body part. This interinclusion of body within time empowers us to focus on and refine the spiritual properties and miraculous functionings of our physical body, as the spiral of the yearly cycle continues to turn on its Divine axis.

Kaved / liver is the body part associated with the month of Teves. The Gemara says, "The liver is the seat of anger" [*Berachos*, 61b]. The word *Kaved* also means 'heavy', and when the liver is not functioning properly, it can make a person heavy, physically and emotionally. Emotional heaviness and feeling bad about oneself leads one to take their personal narratives very seriously. As explained above, this is the greatest cause of anger, and only serves to feed the flames of Tohu, ego and impulsive physicality.

Regarding Pharaoh the Torah says, *Bo el Paroh, ki Ani Hichbad'ti es Libo* / "Come to Pharaoh, for I have hardened his heart" [*Shemos*, 10:1]. The Medrash tells us that Hashem made Pharaoh's heart *Kaved* / heavy, and like a liver, full of blood and anger. He was so caught up in holding onto his story that he would not let the People of Israel leave Egypt even when it was extremely detrimental to him. When did Hashem make the heart of Pharaoh *Kaved*? In the month of the Kaved, the month of Teves [Rabbi Moshe Dovid Valle, *Eis LaChenina*, Bo, p. 115].

The Zohar [3:234a] says that the Kaved is an anatomical representation of Eisav. Eisav and Edom, like the Kaved, are "full of blood" [*Bechoros*, 55a]. Besides being involved in the bloody work of game hunting, Eisav is born covered with red hair. He desires to eat red lentils. His Sar or 'angel' is red, and he is understood to be an embodiment of *Dinim* / harsh judgments, which are from an excess of Gevurah, the 'red' Sefirah.

As discussed previously, when Eisav sees the lentils that Yaakov is cooking, he immediately desires them. The eyes (Ayin) and the liver are also related, since liver disease can often be detected in one's eyes.

The Kav haYashar [Chap. 93] teaches that the Kaved represents *Samm-El*, literally 'the Poison of Hashem', a toxic and destructive force. [The *Techol* / spleen, represents Li'lis / Lilith, who is the feminine aspect of *HaSatan* / the adversary.] Eisav's guiding angel, or *Sar*, is also known as *Samm-El*.

Samm means 'poison'. *Samm-El* thus means, 'Poison of G-d', i.e., the agent of Hashem that delivers Divine toxicity, negativity and chaos. The word *Samm* is spelled Samech (ס), Final Mem (ם), which are both graphically closed letters.* All other letters have openings, and can therefore be circulaters of life force. Samech and Mem represent the closing off of the energy system, stopping the in- and out-flow of life-force, and trapping it in an ouroboric circuit where it stagnates and thus becomes poisonous. Samm-El therefore represents a shutting down of the flow of Divine revelation and blessing, causing the spiritual counterpart of the liver to become toxic.

If there is no fresh revelation in someone's life, their existence will seem bleak and meaningless. If they become increasingly closed off to Divine revelation, then a pull toward the self-centered 'immediate gratification' of *Avodah Zarah* / idolatry or alienating idle worship may arise. Indeed, when people stop believing in their Infinite Source, they do not just believe in *nothing*. They often begin to believe in *anything*. Instead of believing in the *Yesh haAmiti* / True Something, they begin to believe in everything and anything that comes their way, including forces that eventually inject

---

* The *Toldos Yaakov Yoseph* says the negativity of Samm-El can be 'sweetened' or transformed by the power of the Divine name *Sa'al*, one of the 72 three-letter Names of Hashem. [See also Rabbi Moshe Dovid Valle, *Sefer haLikutim* 2.] When we meditate on Sa'al, it can help us overcome the darkness of Kelipah, open the 'closed letters Samech and Mem, and liberate the sparks of purity that were swallowed up and trapped within them. *Toldos Yaakov Yoseph*, Parshas Vayakhel. The name *Sa'al*, is the 45th Name in the 72 Names sequence. These 72 names are derived from the words, *Vayisa Yisrael haLaila...*, "Yisrael traveled by night.." [*Shemos*, 14:19-20], implying that they have the power to override and transform darkness by revealing the light within. The first, last, and first letter from each verse forms a name. These letters are to be pronounced or visualized with their natural vowels, Aleph with a Kamatz, Beis with a Tzeirei, and so forth.

poisons into their soul. Yet, when the closed letters of *Samm* are opened, their root is exposed, and the poison falls away; Samm-El is then revealed to be none other than the beneficial Presence of *E-l* / G-d, working in mysterious ways to bring us back to our Source and center. When we are deeply aligned with E-l, there is no poison, greed, anger, chaos or dis-ease in our system — all is related to as Divine flow. If our eyes are open to see deeply, we can find the Divine Presence everywhere, even within a seemingly negative experience.

This dynamic of closure, expressed within the closed letters of Samech and Final Mem, is also related to the word *Satan*. The three letters that spell *Satan* (Sin-Tes-Nun) are a backwards acronym for *Nitzutzei Teharah Sheba'lah* / sparks of purity that were swallowed up [*Kehilas Yaakov*, Satan]. This teaches us that there is a Divine flow even in dark forces, only it is 'swallowed up', and stopped from being revealed and openly manifest.

Essentially, there are two archetypal sources of the negativity which we continue to generate by our own free choice, and for which we seek long-term detoxification and Tikkun. One of these sources is the *Chet Eitz haDaas* / the sin of eating from (and identifying with) the Tree of Knowledge, and the other is the *Chet haEigel* / the sin of worshipping the Golden Calf. In general, the entire unfolding of history is a Tikkun for these two great misalignments. Correcting the Tree of Knowledge is more of a 'feminine issue', since it was a woman, Chavah / Eve, who suggested that Adam eat prematurely from the Tree. The main instigator of this destructive event, however, was the female demonic force called *Li-lis*. Correcting the Golden Calf is more of a 'male issue', since it was the men, and not the women, who worshipped the idol. The main instigator of this destructive event was the male demonic force, Samm-El. Let us explore in greater depth both of these events, including their effects and their *Tikkunim* / rectifications.

The Chet Eitz haDaas & Its Tikkun:

In the *Chet Eitz haDaas*, Adam and Chavah were told, "From every tree of the Garden you may eat, but from the Tree of the Knowledge of Good and Evil you must not eat...." [*Bereishis*, 2:16-17]. Adam and Chavah were living in the reality of the Tree of Life, completely immersed and identified with Paradise, a space free of duality or opposites, and they were told they should not eat from the 'Tree of Duality of Good and Evil'. Yet, the snake, the external voice of fantasy, tempted Chavah to eat and internalize the perspective of duality: "When the woman saw that the fruit of the Tree was good for food and pleasing to the eye..." [*Bereishis, 3*:6], she ate and then gave it to Adam to eat. As a result of this cosmic and cataclysmic misalignment, Samm-el, in the form of the Snake, was able to draw people into the confusions and illusions of duality, thereby introducing death, shame, exile, power, suffering, work, self-centered lust and the ability to objectify others for one's own personal gain.

Obsessing over temporary, self-oriented physical pleasure blocks true intimacy and open communication with others. Eisav was an embodiment of the snake from the Chet Eitz haDaas. Thus, appropriately, Eisav engraved the image of a snake on his thigh. [See *Sefer Tziyoni*, Toldos, p. 44. *Shaloh haKodesh*, Torah shebeKsav, Tzon Yoseph, 12. Interestingly, Chushim — who killed Eisav, as mentioned — in numerical value is 358, as is the word *Nachash* / snake and *Moshiach* / Messiah.] The thigh, a euphemism for the procreative organ, is where Yaakov was injured when he wrestled with the Sar of Eisav. This indicates that Yaakov struggled with physical cravings as well, stemming from his inner Eisav [see *Rabbeinu Bachya*, Bereishis, 32:25]. This is not unusual, as the energy of Eisav and the Snake are part of the human DNA. What is notable is that Yaakov succeeded in his struggle to overcome and integrate his lower nature in a healthy balance of holy relationship. As Yaakov was victorious, he opened a channel for our successful Tikkun in this area, as well.

The entire process of *Gilgulim* / soul-reincarnations across lifetimes, is all due to the original separation of Adam and Chavah and the splintering of the Unified Soul of humanity. Adam and Chavah's shared soul is the collective and universal soul from which all human souls emanate. [See *Sha'ar haGilgulim*, Hakdamah 12. *Shiur Komah*, 2. Tanya, *Iggeres haKodesh*, 7. Note: *Medrash Rabbah*, Shemos, 40:3. *Tanchumah*, Ki Tissa, 12.] As all souls were contained within this one primordial soul, once they ate from the Tree of the Knowledge of Duality, sparks within this soul were scattered throughout all worlds, times, peoples and places.

The eating of the Tree of Knowledge in Eden caused a shrinking, a breaking apart of the one great body or soul of humanity into myriads of scattered sparks of light. The once unified body of humanity became pixelated, shattering into countless pieces. Each shard became another specific and finite soul-spark. Ever since then, the purpose of the process of reincarnation is to restore the integral wholeness of the One Root Soul. One by one, through a series of lives and Tikkunim, all sparks become brilliant and reintegrated again. When a person lives his or her life and completely expresses their soul-spark, their particular shard of soul is *Zahir / illumined*. After this soul completes its journey through physical life, the now illuminated soul-spark returns to the great Body/Soul of Adam and Chavah, adding to the cosmic Tikkun and at-one-ment of the primordial image of humanity.

The Chet haEigel & Its Tikkun:

While the Chet Eitz haDaas needs universal fixing, and all worlds and all people need to participate in its Tikkun, the cataclysmic event which is more indigenous to *Klal Yisrael* / the Community of Israel, is the *Chet haEigel haZahav* / the Sin of the Golden Calf. This sin immediately followed the greatest revelation in history, the Giving of the Torah at Mount Sinai. This Cheit is the second archetypal source of negativity in the world, and it comes from an obsessive 'need' to worship an image, to connect to *Avodah Zarah* / alienating worship or false power. Samm-El is part of the G-d-given power that creates the illusion that the world exists independently and separate from its Source, and then attempts to draw people into a desire for independent power. Relying on any power other than Hashem actively obscures the revelation of Divine Oneness in the world.

Mitzvos, which are gifted specifically to Klal Yisrael through the revelation of Torah, are acts of 'connection', arrows or bridges that connect us in an overt way with Hashem. Every Mitzvah we do reveals a deeper bond between us and our Creator. This is part of the Tikkun of the Chet haEigel: to always be looking to connect to the 'Who', the One who is commanding the Mitzvah. Intimate connection with the Divine is the existential ends to which the Mitzvos are the behavioral and cognitive means. The focus of these actions is not just on *what* we do, rather *Who* we do them for, to Whom we connect while doing them. This way, we never confuse the Message for the messenger, and we are always connecting our finite life with the infinite Source of All Life.

The first of these two meta-events, eating from the Tree of Dualistic Knowledge, is more universal and the second, worshipping the Golden Calf, more indigenous, but both in their own way give strength to Tohu, the power of 'the other side'. Even though there is really only One 'Side', One Reality, the illusion of duality, separation and alienation can hold powerful sway over us. For this reason the idea of 'two' appears in the text numerous times when Yaakov is about to encounter Eisav, indicating the Torah's desire to include Eisav (Tohu) within Yaakov (the world of Tikkun). The meta-purpose for this inclusion and unification is for them to journey together towards Moshiach and the Ultimate Redemption. It turns out in the text, however, that Eisav is not yet ready for this journey, and so Yaakov tells him, "Let my master (Eisav) go ahead before his servant (Yaakov), and I will move at my own slow pace, until I come to my master, at Seir." This means eventually Yaakov will join Eisav [33:14, *Rashi*], when Eisav is more prepared. Later, when Yaakov sends gifts to Eisav he sends "two hundred female goats, twenty male goats, two hundred ewes, and twenty rams" [32:15]. Yaakov also divides his camp into two [*Ibid*, 8]. By reaching out to Eisav where he is, in his world of duality and conflict, Yaakov gently prepares him to acknowledge and accept true unity.

Besides the two root causes of the influence of Tohu and Kelipah mentioned above, the basic idea of Tohu is that there are always at least two clashing forces involved. The presence of ego always implies two-ness: a me and you, an us and them. 'Two' is the world of 'Tohu'. [These words even seem to be phonetically related.] In the spiritual root of Tohu, the 'world' that precedes our world of Tikkun, there are two separate columns of Sefiros, without the mediating third pillar; in fact, all of the ten Sefiros are separate, there is thus no inter-inclusion or harmony. Yaakov, however, represents 'three-ness', being the third of the Patriarchs; this introduces the middle pillar. The number 3 is 1 + 2, thus the paradigm of 'three' includes and harmonizes the dichotomous paradigms of oneness and two-ness. This is the power of Tikkun, to reconcile clashing opposites, to resolve contradiction, to absorb and elevate paradox. As the embodiment of the World of Tikkun, Yaakov wishes to absorb the two-ness and conflict of Eisav into Tikkun. His mission is to reach out to the unbridled lights of Tohu and contextualize them within the broad vessels of Tikkun; to unify the material world with its spiritual source, in a more integrated and expansive identity.

In summary, the *Kaved* / liver can become a source of separateness and negativity if it incites the body to pursue self-gratification, false love, brute force, or corrupted power. However, the liver also has tools to process and transform these Tohu energies into passionate generosity, holy intimacy and compassionate power, when directed by Torah

ELEMENT

*T*HERE ARE FOUR PRIMARY ELEMENTS, FOUR FUNDAMENTAL building blocks of creation: fire, air, water and earth. Each month is associated with one of these four elements. However, it is important to note that while manifesting physically, these elements are also meant to be understood in a much more metaphysical sense as well, as they represent numerous properties, qualities, and correspondences.*

---

* For a more in-depth exploration of these elements and their relationship to the Hebrew calendar, please see the introductory volume of this series: *The Spiral of Time: Unraveling the Yearly Cycle.*

Teves corresponds to the element of Earth. Earth is cold and dry, as this month is the peak of the winter months. This harsh coldness and dryness is a reflection of the spiritually harsh nature of the month, being the month of the siege of Jerusalem, and thus the beginning of the destruction of the Temple.

As explored earlier, those who were born under the astrological sign of Capricorn have a deep connection with the element of earth and the material realm; this can either inspire positive or negative character traits.

'Earth' is also the quality of earthiness, a connection to the 'now', the immediacy of the moment. In this respect the element of earth resonates with Eisav's traits. On the other hand, the earth is steady, solid, and unmoving, unlike fire which leaps upward, or wind which moves about, or water which flows from above to below [*Ta'anis*, 7a]. This steadiness alludes to the World of Tikkun and provides the antidote to Eisav's erratic unsteadiness and the chaotic power of Tohu.

The unmoving solidity of earth alludes to the unchanging Divine Essence, that which redemptively reconciles and unites materiality and spirituality, resolving seemingly intractable conflicts. This unification is an antidote to the events of this month which led to the destruction of the Temple, the bridge between Heaven and earth.

TORAH PORTIONS

Over the course of a month, 4-5 weekly Torah portions are read by the community. These individual portions can be combined and viewed as a single unit based on the particular month in which they are most commonly read. Indeed, one finds, when viewing the *Parshas* through this calendrical lens, that an astounding array of thematic elements consistent with the spiritual energy of the month are revealed.

In Teves we read the portions of Miketz through Shemos, which tell of the beginning of the Egyptian Exile. We begin with the descent of Yoseph's brothers into Egypt, and end with the death of Yoseph.

The Magid of Koznitz asks why, from the portion of Miketz through VaYigash until half-way through VaYechi, do we not find the Name of Hashem (*Havayah*) even once? This seems quite unusual. The Magid answers: it is because the Name *Hashem* represents *Rachamim* / Divine Compassion. The portion of Miketz describes the beginning of the Exile: Pharaoh dreams of the great Famine, which eventually causes Yaakov and his family to descend to Egypt, which results in the long and oppressive Exile, in which Hashem's presence is concealed from us. These Torah portions are saturated with *Din* / harsh judgment, and there is very little revealed Rachamim in them. Consequently, this particular Divine Name is not mentioned during these Parshas.

In the month of Teves we also experienced the beginning of the first post-Sinai exile. This was the Babylonian Exile, starting with the destruction of the First *Beis haMikdash* / Temple, and which eventually drove us from the Land of Israel, the place where our indigenous spirituality was united with the material realm in a most revealed manner. The siege on the Temple began on the tenth day of Teves, which is therefore a fast day, to commemorate the initiation of the collective trauma of exile.

Despite this heaviness, these Torah portions also teach us how to neutralize and sweeten Din and convert it into Rachamim. Yoseph is a clear example of this 'sweetening' process. Even as Yoseph was rejected by his brothers and sold into slavery, he is ultimately the one who is able to see the positive aspects within the entire saga. When he reunites his family, he reveals that his exile was for a higher purpose — to serve a as a source of sustenance for his people, both physically and spiritually.

Yoseph specifically shows us how to detach from and transform a narrative of anger. He had good reason to be angry at his brothers for selling him into slavery and essentially exiling him from the family, and yet he does not dwell at all on thoughts of judgement or revenge. Instead, he has the vision to look beyond the immediate appearance of things; he clearly sees that everything that happened had a Divine purpose. Even though his brothers wronged him terribly, he is therefore able to tell them: "It was not you who sent me here, but Hashem" [*Bereishis*, 45:9]. "Indeed, you intended evil against me, [but] Hashem designed it for good, in order to bring this all about to keep a great populace alive" [*Bereishis*, 50:20].

Our Sages tell us we should learn to overcome anger from the example of Yoseph. In the words of the Alter Rebbe: "So, too, in matters 'between man and his fellow-man'. As soon as there rises from his heart to his mind any animosity, hatred, or anger, G-d forbid, he will bar them from his mind and will *refuse to even think of them*. On the contrary, his mind will prevail over and dominate the feelings of his heart to do the exact opposite of that which the heart *desires*, namely, to conduct himself toward his fellow with the quality of kindness, without being provoked into anger, G-d forbid, or to take revenge in kind, G-d forbid (even without anger). On the contrary, he repays offenders with favors, as taught in the Zohar [*Zohar* 1, p. 201a], that we should learn from the example of Yoseph's conduct with his brothers" [*Tanya*, Chap. 12].

It is interesting to note, given the network of energies, emotions and ideas associated with Teves, that Yoseph also overcame overwhelming temptations. Indeed, as recorded in the Torah, Yoseph's superhuman power to resist the allures and advances of Potiphar's wife, even when given the opportunity, indicates to the Sages that Yoseph had refined himself on this most foundational level to an astonishing degree. This Tikkun of *Yesod* / psycho-carnal energy is connected to Yoseph's ability to overcome his 'valid' anger and forgive his brothers. Anger and lust are in many ways related energies and impulses — aggressive, fiery, consuming, and potentially chaotic. Refining the capacity for permitted, meaningful, respectful, intimate relationships is a cornerstone of whole-system anger management. However, Yoseph provides an example of going well beyond mere management of such primal energies, as his story expresses a rare ability to purify and harness these deep wellsprings, redirecting their flow into positive and productive channels.

Yoseph was able to channel the raw sensations of arousal and anger, focusing them into a positive path of Tikkun, rather than a destructive path of Tohu. Instead of responding to Potiphar's wife or his brothers with the chaos of impulsive or reactive behavior, he becomes the great sustainer of the entire Land of Egypt in the years of famine through his measured behavior. When we do not unconsciously react to the sensation of anger, we too can funnel the powerful energy into ingenuity and creativity, and become a channel of healthy sustenance and loving-kindness for our family and wider world.

SEASONS OF THE YEAR

THE SEASONAL QUALITIES OF EACH MONTH ARE INTRICATELY related with the spiritual qualities of that month. When daylight lasts for either longer or shorter times, different kinds of spiritual light are being revealed on a subtle level. The physical experiences of spring are external expressions of an internal reality emanating during that time, such as the vital pulse of new life and growth. All dark and dank months reflect an energy of corresponding spiritual 'coldness', stimulating us to seek warmth. People tend to keep to themselves when winter begins and are more outgoing when summer starts. All of these psycho-physical weather patterns reflect deeper spiritual truths, as the mind-body complex is a reflection of the metaphysical qualities of the soul and spiritual realm.

Teves is one of the most intense and 'unholy' months of the year, teaches the Zohar. After Moshe, who represents goodness, was born, he was hidden for three months. These three months correspond to Teves, Tamuz and the first half of Av; the times in the year in which the light of goodness is not manifest in a revealed manner [*Zohar* 2, *Shemos*, 12a]. Teves, the coldest month, and Tamuz, the hottest month, are the only two months that are, as discussed, entirely 'under the domain of Eisav'. As such, there is a draw toward Eisav-like behaviors and reactions to these climatic extremes. The cold of Teves specifically leads people to an increased desire for physical warmth. This is why it is described as a month in which "body takes pleasure in body."

During the previous month, Kislev, the small measure of increased daylight stimulated renewed hope. Although winter is at its peak during Teves, and the darkness can lead one deeper into feelings of depression and retreat, the recent infusion of light and hope of Kislev provided an opening to reconnect with and be open to others. Thus the 'hibernation' that began in Cheshvan is beginning to recede into the past, and now during Teves one seeks relationship with others — and specifically to retreat from the cold in the warmth of another person.

Normally, in Teves, the time of sunset and of lighting Shabbos candles does not change for two weeks in a row. In this sense, time seemingly stands still during these dreary days. Daylight neither increases nor decreases; we feel as though we are not moving further toward summer nor toward winter. This lack of movement can be psychologically disconcerting. Even when the days get shorter and darker and colder, at least there is movement. Whenever we are moving up or down there is a sense of change, the quality of being alive. When there is no perceivable change or stimulation, however, life can seem stagnant and empty. When the days seem still, and we light the candle at the exact same time two weeks in a row, there is an eerie sensation like when the EKG signal goes flat.

Teves starts with the letter Tes, the ninth letter of the Aleph-Beis. Tes represents something hidden, as its form is coiled in upon itself (ט). It is the least common letter in the entire Torah; from among all the 22 letters, Tes is thus the most 'concealed' letter. In fact, all of the letters were inscribed in the first set of *Luchos / tablets*, besides the letter Tes [*Baba Kama*, 55a. See also: *Pesikta Zutrasa*, Devarim, 9b]. Numerically, Tes is 9. In general, 9 is a mysterious number. There is a mystical tradition that the ninth verse in every *Parshah* / portion of the Torah has a much deeper meaning than how it appears on the surface. [*Mei haShiloach*, Parshas Balak and Parshas Devarim.] In a Torah scroll there is an empty space of nine letters between one Torah portion and the next. 'Nine' thus represents the empty space between the fullness of the words of the Torah, the white space, the *Ayin* / no-thingness.

Ayin is the unmoving state of transcendent non-being. *Yesh* / separate existence is movement: ascending or descending, getting colder and darker or warmer and lighter, feeling better or feeling worse. When there is no stimulation of thought or sensation, our attention is drawn inward toward our experience of Ayin, our inner stillness and silence. Yet, the vast emptiness and timelessness stillness of Ayin can be very disorienting, and therefore our minds usually create chatter to bridge the chasm, to fill the emptiness with images and fill the silence with sound. However, when we encounter this chasm in our consciousness we have an opportunity for a most profound realization. Instead of reactively covering over the space with thoughts and activities, we can let go of our narratives and become present with the seemingly bleak emptiness, transforming it into a fertile void. Eventually the experience of silence is sweetened and we may be able to taste the spiritual pleasure of intimacy with our own inner stillness and stability. Activation of this awareness enables us to relate to others on a deeper level as well, revealing the relational and social impacts of inner spiritual work.

The antidote for the negative 'emptiness' of Teves, which is the *Ayin of Kelipah*, is the holy no-thingness, the *Ayin of Kedusha*. The Ayin of Kelipah is the source and beginning of all destruction — it is that which rendered the Beis haMikdash a 'no-thing'. We begin to activate the antidote when we learn to welcome and be present with silence and stillness, as well as with noise and strong sensations. This unflinching presence allows for a genuine self-encounter, and cultivates our ability to navigate and balance our multiple dimensions of Yesh and Ayin. We ultimately become able to integrate our numerous desires, yearnings, wants, thoughts, and feelings within our inner stillness, silence, self-acceptance and spiritual emptiness. Thus we include our beingness within our non-beingness. This inclusion is synonymous with a shift into *Etzem*-consciousness or 'Essence', the infinite context that transcends and includes both our Yesh and Ayin, simultaneously dissolving and weaving them together into a dynamic unity.

Yesh is a fullness of self, and is thus, when unchecked, related to our entanglements in ego; Ayin is an emptiness of self and is thus, when properly directed, related to our transcendence of ego. The objective is to live in harmony with both Yesh and Ayin, and not to be locked into either polarity. Etzem-consciousness allows us to function as an ego, but one that is transparent to Ayin. In Etzem-consciousness our 'I' is intimately united and included within the ultimate, essential 'I' of Hashem. This is a one-to-One, 'body-to-Body' or 'self to Self' encounter, similar to marital intimacy. The *Halachah* / Torah guideline for marital intimacy is to have no intervening clothing between partners [*Kesuvos*, 48a. *Tikkunei Zohar*, Tikkun 58]. In the Divine intimacy of Etzem-consciousness, there are no intervening *Gilu'im* / outer manifestations or garments, for "body takes pleasure in Body," as it were. This is the deepest meaning in the non-movement of the sunset times which occurs during this month, as movements are but Gilu'im, veils which attract but also conceal. Etzem-consciousness is the best antidote to the selfishness that can arise during this month. When self-centeredness arises we can amplify our consciousness of the Divine Self, the Etzem, that which simultaneously transcends and includes all of reality, our stillness and our movement, our Ayin and Yesh.

The Tzemach Tzedek, the Third Chabad Rebbe, comments on this type of intimate union, the total "body to Body" connection: in Divine union, when there is a higher kiss with the lips, angelic beings are created. This kiss ripples through all worlds below; the Supernal Mind unifies within itself and angels are born. When two bodies kiss and unite, however, souls are born. A kiss is a unification on the level of mind and heart, but only in full intimacy, the unification of body to body, are souls conceived and birthed. Thus essence-to-essence union on this plane is a mirror image of our essence unifying with the *Etzem* / Essence of Hashem, the root of Souls [*Derech Mitzvosechah*, Mitzvas Peru uRevu]. When an *Av* / father

(*Av*=3), and *Eim* / mother (*Eim*=41) unite, they become 44, which is the numerical value of *Yeled* / child — spelled Yud Lamed Dalet. This is the essence and archetype of all spousal, positive and generative intimacy, as opposed to purely self-serving or destructive arousal which is ultimately a dead-end.

THE HOLIDAY OF THE MONTH

"For everything there is an appointed time" (*Koheles*, 3:1). In other words, everything happens according to Divine timing (Rebbe RaYatz, *Sefer haMa'amorim*, tof/shin/aleph, p. 59). Our Sages tell us that when we left Egypt, it was the appointed time for such liberation. This means not only that it occurred in the historically appropriate time, but also at the right time of year — the season best suited for this expression of Redemption [*Mechilta deRabbi Yishmael*, Bo, 16, on the verse in Tehillim, 68:7]. This is the same principle behind every *Yom Tov*: the narrative and observance of each celebration or fast reflects and refracts the light of the natural world through a spiritual lens.

Furthermore, in the months that contain a *Yom Tov* / holiday, that *Yom Tov* embodies and encapsulates the energy of the entire month in condensed form. In a month that does not have a major holiday, that absence is also an expression of the unique energy of the month.

The Tenth of Teves is a fast day commemorating the *Haschalas Puraniyus* / beginning of hardship, specifically the beginning of the Babylonian Exile. The siege of Jerusalem began on this day and this led to the eventual destruction of the First Temple and the first exile of the People of Israel since becoming a nation. Once there was a siege, the eventual destruction of everything else was just an actualization of that negative potential which was born on the Tenth of Teves. This is the deeper reason why we still commemorate the day of the siege: it was the beginning of the downfall that still affects us today.

When a city is under siege there is a blocking of the movement of people, resources and ideas, into and out of its walls. Yerushalayim was the seat of the Divine Presence revealed here on earth, especially during the time of the First Beis haMikdash, as it was said: "From Tziyon emanates the Torah...." [*Micah* 4:2, *Yeshayahu*, 2:3]. Yerushalayim was, so to speak, the 'giver' of the living flow of Torah and Kedushah to the 'recipient', the rest of Israel and the whole world. The siege impeded this flow, blocking the healthy exchange into and out of Yerushalayim.* This caused the perception of *Pirud* / separation within the unity that was revealed through the Beis haMikdash. Such an entrapment of Light, as within the enclosed letters Samach and Final Mem, as discussed, allows the 'Oth-

---

* There is a tradition that Avraham passed away during the month of Teves

er Side' to eventually wreak its havoc and destruction.* This is the deeper reason for the sadness and intensity of the Tenth of Teves. It was on this day that the world was seemingly cut off from the living flow of Kedusha and *Kevod* / glory of Hashem. The Tikkun

---

[*Sefer Karnayim*, Ma'amar 6. Note by R. Shamshon of Ostropol. *Dan Yadin*, 3. See also *Beis Yisrael* (Gur) Chanukah, 1953]״טבת״ ר״ת למפרע בשיבה טובה ״תקבר. Avraham, the first of the Avos, embodies Chesed, giving, loving, and goodness — and he passed away in this month. The Alter Rebbe also passed away in Teves. Each of the seven Chabad Rebbes especially embodied one of the seven emotive Sefiros. As the first Rebbe, the Alter Rebbe too represents Chesed. Alternatively, the Gemara says Avraham passed away in Nisan or in Tishrei [*Rosh Hashanah*, 10b-11a]. If so, this may mean that he was buried in Teves [*Regel Yeshara* by the Bnei Yissaschar, Ma'areches Tes, 15]. It could also mean that he died on a day within Nisan or Tishrei that corresponds inwardly to the month of Teves, as these months are 'head' months and therefore include all the months of the year within them. In any case, these phenomena point to the dynamic of Teves in which there is a blockage, a holding back, or a 'burial' of the flow of Chesed. This dynamic is pointedly expressed in the Siege.

---

*The Gemara says, *Samach v'Mem b'Neis Hayu Omdim* / "the Samach and the (Final) Mem stood by means of a miracle" [*Shabbos*, 104a]. This teaching refers to the *Luchos*, the 'tablets' of sapphire, into which the Ten Sayings were carved. Each letter was carved all the way through from one side to the other. Since the letters Samach and Mem are closed shapes, the pieces inside the letters must have been suspended in mid air, and thus it is said that they "stood by means of a miracle". These two letters therefore are characterized by mystery and hiddenness, alluding to their power to enclose and conceal the Divine flow.

In the beginning of the book of Vayikra, there is a small Aleph. A large Aleph represents *Eleph* / 1,000. A small Aleph represents 1. Following the *Chet haEgel* / sin of the Golden Calf, and the subsequent smashing of the Luchos, Moshe lost 1,000 'lights', thus Vayikra, has a small Aleph. Why specifically 1,000 lights? In the Luchos there are 22 final Mems and there are two Samachs. Mem is 40; 22 x 40 = 880. Samach is 60; 2 x 60 = 120. These two sums, 880 + 160 = 1,000. As above, since the letters Samach and Mem are closed shapes, the pieces inside the letters in the Luchos must have been suspended in mid-air. Therefore, when Moshe breaks the Luchos, all the letters are smashed into smaller shards, except the Samach and the Mem 'disappear', and are hidden away.

for this entire gestalt is achieved through refining one's capacity for intimacy in order to activate the principle of "body takes pleasure in body" in an elevated and uplifting way. This essential unity with the Divine Self ensures proper flow, movement, intake and output of energy, between the Giver and ourselves, the receivers.

Based on all this, the Tenth of Teves is one of the most intense fasts of the year. According to Tanach, it seems that all other fasts could be performed on any day of the respective month [*Minchas Chinuch*, Mitzvah 370]: "the fast of the Fourth (month), the fast of the Fifth (month)...."[*Zecharyah*, 8:19]. However, with regard to the Tenth of Teves, the day itself is singled out: "the tenth day of the month...."[*Yechezkel*, 24:1-2].

So potent is the Tenth of Teves that it is the only fast that we do not postpone when it falls out on Friday [Orach Chayim, *Magen Avraham* 550:4]. In some ways this is similar to Yom Kippur, another fast-day that falls out on the 10th of a month. When Yom Kippur falls out on Shabbos, the Mitzvah of fasting on Yom Kippur pushes aside the Mitzvah of eating on Shabbos. R. David Avudaraham writes that if the Tenth of Teves were to fall out on Shabbos [which it never does, as our fixed calendar prevents this from happening], it too would potentially push aside the Mitzvah of eating on Shabbos. [*Hilchos Ta'anis*. Although see *Orach Chayim, Beis Yoseph* 550. Note *Rashi*, Megilah 5a (Shu't, *Shoel Umeishiv*, Mahadura Kama 3, 179) Rambam, *Hilchos Ta'aniyos*, 5:5.] This is a very unusual idea, as on all fast days besides Yom Kippur, Shabbos dominates and pushes off the fast day to the adjacent Thursday or Sunday. The fast of the Tenth of Teves is seemingly too important to push off.

A simple reason for this is that all other fast days commemorate a particular event in history. Although that event occurred on a specific date, the date itself is not as essential as the general event being commemorated. We can still remember those events on an adjacent day. Therefore even the fast of the Ninth of Av, which commemorates the destructions of both Temples on that day, is moved to Sunday whenever the Ninth falls out on Shabbos. With regard to Yom Kippur, and apparently the Tenth of Teves, the day itself is considered essential, the respective fasts are not merely commemorations of specific events from the past, but expressions of the day itself in the present moment.

The fact that the Tenth of Teves is as 'un-movable' as Yom Kippur is demonstrated in the Torah's use of the words regarding the siege: *b'Etzem haYom haZeh* / in the essence of this day [*Yechezkel*, 24:2]. This is also the exact phrase used regarding Yom Kippur [*Vayikra*, 23:29]. The respective fasts are thus about the 'day' itself, both Yom Kippur and the Tenth of Teves.

On a deeper level, the Tenth of Teves, like Yom Kippur, is an *Etzem haYom* / a day of Etzem, a time of intimately knowing and uniting the unmoving aspect of Ayin and the dynamic movement of Yesh into One Infinite reality. When our essence is one with the Essence of Hashem in a conscious, revealed way, we give birth to the Soul of Redemption. In Essence consciousness, the *Din* / concealment and hardship of exile is included and transformed within the deeper paradigm of Redemption.

May this come about speedily in our days.

☾

PRACTICE:
Taking the Time to Think about our Relationships

*I*N THIS MONTH, AS AN INTIMATE AWARENESS OF THE PHYSICAL body comes to the fore, it is very helpful to reflect upon the nature of 'physical relationships' in our lives, and our relationships with others in general. How is your relationship with your spouse? How are your relationships with your parents, siblings, children, co-workers, friends, teachers and community members? Are your interactions and exchanges predominantly self-serving and 'all about you'? Do you tend to objectify or instrumentalize others, or view relationships in a purely transactional manner? Are you working to improve your relationships? What is Hashem calling you to change, or maintain for the sake of your physical refinement and spiritual growth, as well as that of all others you come into contact with?

Are you overly-possessive in your relationships? Is your focus entirely on yourself or are you also able to consider the needs and boundaries of the other? Are your connections with others based on what you are selfishly receiving? Or are they based on your desire to be selflessly giving? Or is there actually a healthy balance of giving and receiving? Think about the various ways that you could more consciously and compassionately balance your relationships.

Are you proactively grateful in your life, or do you take other people for granted? Do you ever feel entitled in your relationships? Do you ever act callously or express yourself at the expense of others? Do you tend to lash out in anger towards those with whom you are closest? Do you struggle with a 'Tohu' quality of greed for immediate gratification? When someone does not gratify or satisfy you, what is your response?

Take time out right now to contemplate the deeper purpose in your relationships and discover the potential for positivity in your modes of human connection. What can you do today to cultivate patience, gratitude, heartfelt compassion or mindful communication? How can you clarify your Tohu emotions and harness them for Tikkun and acts of goodness?

KAVANAH / *Mindful Intention & Practice*

Our sages teach that immersing your body in a *Mikvah* / pool of living water is a Tikkun for anger. As explained at length in this volume, Teves deals with the *Chush* / sense of anger, and when one's anger is not harnessed properly, one becomes buried under the weight of their narrative, like something stuck in the frozen earth.

Whether one is stagnating in the cold rigidity of a relentless attachment to one's narrative, or flaring up in anger, one needs the antidote of immersing in a Mikvah, a ritual pool of natural water.

Ka'as / anger, in its numerical value, equals = 150 (Chaf/20 + Ayin/70 + Samach/60 = 150). We can add 1 for the word itself, yielding 151 (The reason why the 'word' itself is also counted, writes the Shaloh, is because most people who are angry use *words* to spew their anger. *Sha'ar HaOysyos*, Kedusha, 12).

A Torah word for 'anger' or wrath is *Kanah*, which in numerical value is 151 (Kuf/100 + Nun/50 + Aleph/1 = 151). *Mikvah*, in numerical value, is also 151 (Mem/40 + Kuf/100 + Vav/6 + Hei/5 = 151). This suggests an intrinsic connection between overcoming the detrimental effects of anger and immersion in the Mikvah, suggesting it is through Mikvah that a person can he healed of their anger [*Sha'ar Ruach haKodesh*, Tikkun 15. *Kehilas Yaakov*, Ka'as. p. 755].*

---

* As an aside, it is helpful to remember that a numerical equivalence is not mere coincidence (of course nothing in this universe is), and the link between the two equivalent words is often quite profound. Their numerical correlation is an external indication of their inner relationship, however, and not the source or the foundation of their link. A numerical equivalence does not automatically suggest a cosmological or theological relationship, rather, the numerology is an outward expression of a deeper cosmological truth that is already present, although possibly not revealed [Ramban, *Sefer HaGeulah*, in the beginning. Rabbeinu Bachya, *Kad Kemach*, Tzitzis. *Shomer Emunim HaKadmon*, 1, 20-23]. Sometimes the numerical equivalency is the key that unlocks a secret garden.

In anger a person self-centeredly cuts himself off from the Source of all life. Anger is related to idol worship, as it is rooted in a form of self-worship. Anger is thus a transgression between you and your Creator, and by extension between you and Hashem's Creation.

On an interpersonal level, acting out in anger is most damaging to the recipient of your anger. But, on a deeper level, acting out in anger is not only harmful to others but also to oneself. Anger ends up leading a person to do, say, and mentally entertain things that they normally would not. "One who becomes angry is as if he lit the fires of *Gehenom* / hell…." [*Tikkunei Zohar*, Tikkun 48. See *Nedarim*, 22a]. As a result, all forms of torment, anguish, and misery are opened and ignited in the wake of anger.

If something irritates an angry person slightly, he explodes into flames. This is because his habitual response pattern has deadened his nervous system, making him cold and dry, like highly flammable kindling. The life-giving waters of the Mikvah 'moisten' us and extinguish the hellish fires of anger.

Not only does the fire of expressed anger harm the people around us, but us as well. Anger burns down a person's promising future and true potential. When a person is angry they deny themselves access to the person they can truly become. A person who has been singed by anger feels dessicated, small, narrow, constricted and limited. Because this is how he experiences himself, he projects the same image upon all people, as well as the world around him. Such a person begins to feel that the whole world is out to get them, it is thus a bad world, with no hope or possibility. Predictably, one's dreams evaporate.

"An angry person should not pray." [See *Eiruvin*, 65a. See Tosefos, ad loc, for the 'Biblical' source. *Tur*, Orach Chayim Siman 98. Nowadays, one should nonetheless pray: *Mechaber*, Siman 98:2.] This is because, on a deeper level, he cannot pray due to his self-centeredness, as expressed through his anger, which as mentioned is likened to idol worship. He is therefore not open to the conditions of prayer.

After many years of not seeing his beloved son Yoseph, and thinking he was no longer alive, Yaakov said, "I never *Philalti* that I would ever see your face again" [*Bereishis*, 48:11]. What does *Philalti* mean in this context? Rashi interprets Yaakov's statement to imply: "I was so devastated by your absence that I never would have *filled my heart* with the thought that I would ever see your face again." As such, the Hebrew word *leHispalel* / to pray, from the same root as *Philalti*, means to consciously fill our hearts and minds with thoughts or dreams of what we desire to see in this world. It is to envision a world that is healed and perfected, to hope, to dream. It is to imagine a sick person becoming healed, a broken-hearted person feeling whole, and ultimately, the entire world rejoicing in exquisite wholeness with the coming of Moshiach. But when a person is angry, everything seems gloomy, morbid, depressing, without *Chayus* / life, or any possibility for a brighter future. For this reason, he cannot pray. Without a spiritually healthy understanding of Hashem's world, one cannot pray.

"My eye is dimmed from anger" [*Tehilim*, 6:8. 31:10. *Iyov*, 17:7]. In anger a person's vision is muddied; he cannot evaluate a situation correctly, and so his actions are reactionary. He is enclosed within his narrow tunnel vision; his consciousness is blocked. A wise person forgets his wisdom in anger, and a prophet loses his Divine intuition [*Pesachim*, 66b]. Whoever you are, and whatever level you are on, you regress in anger. Everything of value is lost. "An angry person", say our sages, "is left with nothing other than his anger" [*Kidushin*, 41a]. For example, if a wise person becomes angry, his clarity of thought is clouded and there is no wisdom left. Such loss of wisdom can be understood quite literally. When in the grips of anger, the body produces more adrenaline, giving the body more physical strength and vitality to fight, but less blood flows to the brain. Since our brains gets less oxygen, our thinking is less clear.

Anger damages vision by creating habits which make it increasingly difficult for a person to see what is really happening in front of him. Over time, he no longer notices that he is viewing the world through the lens of anger. Everything and everyone looks like they are scheming to threaten his existence.

An angry person becomes isolated and separated from other individuals, and an angry group separates itself from other groups. When a person feels justifiably angry because of what a particular person did to him, his blaming and counter-attack cut him off from having open relationships with others. Everyone senses his instability and volatility, and instinctually stays away in distaste or fear. Devastatingly, this can happen with those he is closest to — his spouse, parents, children.

"There is no friendship or companionship in anger" [R. Yedaya haPenini (?-1305) *Mivchar haPninim*, 18:2]. In the experience of anger one feels extremely isolated and lonely. No one seems to be 'on his side' and everyone and everything is conspiring against him. Such deep isolation, if not dealt with, will lead to paranoia and mistrust. Anger can cause a person to lose his trusted friends. Ultimately, anger isolates and alienates a person even from himself, and that is the most devastating effect of all.

Before long, habitual, unchecked or unrectified anger mutates into lifelessness and despondency. Anger directed inwardly can become the source of deep depression. Depression can be understood as 'anger without enthusiasm'. Once one sinks down into the frigid cold of depression it becomes that much more difficult to be lifted up into a state of *Chayus* / life, warmth, connectivity, hope or freedom.

"For an angry person, his life is not life" [*Pesachim*, 113b]. His anger eventually leads to a type of inner 'death' and *Tumah* / ritual impurity, cut off from others, from oneself, and from life itself. This leaves a person bereft of vitality, energy, a sense of goodness and appreciation of being alive.

When the Chayus of the person leaves, they are bitter, hopeless and unmoveable. They see the world around them in the same way. This is not merely a psychological phenomenon, but also a deep spiritual malady. The holy Zohar tells us that a person who is angry 'loses his soul' [*Zohar* 2, p. 182b. *Sha'ar haGilgulim*, haKdamah 5]. Every negative act affects one particular area in the body. For example, lying affects the mouth, and seeing negative imagery affects the eyes. However, anger breaches the soul itself, and the entire soul departs when a person is under the siege of anger [*Sha'ar Ruach haKodesh*, p, 33].

When a person becomes angry their face turns red, and perhaps other colors, but, then most noticeably, they become pale or white. This change of facial color, from a metaphysical point of view, is an external representation of an internal depletion and loss of spirit and soul [*Maor vaShemesh*, Parshas Tazriah]. There is a tangible effect on the body when the soul, the inner-life force, leaves due to anger. The face and body become like a ruined city.

Therefore, what is needed is a total purification and thorough transformation of this Tumah, deadness and stagnation, into a condition of *Tehara* / ritual purity, vitality, fluidity, unity and possibility. This occurs through immersion in a Mikvah, a physical-psychological-spiritual gift of the Torah that restores the movement and openness of a life-affirming mindset, and allows one to regain his lost soul [*Reishis Chochmah*, Sha'ar haAhavah, 11]. In these tranquil living waters, one can be infused with *Chayus* and hope. His unyielding stiffness can return to fluidity, flexibility and aliveness.

When we are hard, inflexible and rigid, we are consorting with death and Tumah. When we mingle with the waters of Taharah, we become softer and more water-like; we shed our shell of deadness and germinate a new sense of aliveness and purity. Water is the source of life, and the Mikvah reconnects us to the Source of Life.

As we now understand, the primary reason people become angry is because life violates their expectations and perceptions of what is and what should be. If you buy a beautiful pair of shoes and go out to show them off, and as you are strutting about a passing car splashes an oily puddle on them, you might become angry.

A wealthy person is "one who has a bathroom next to his table"

[*Shabbos*, 25b]. Wealth is joy, as our sages tell us, "Who is wealthy? One who is joyous *with what he has*" [*Avos*, 4:1]. In addition to the image of luxury (for previous generations) of having a "bathroom next to the table", there is a deeper meaning for us. A wealthy, or joyous, person is someone who is as easy with his "outtake" (restroom) as his "intake" (table). He is as easy with gathering in as he is with letting go. He is flexible with life, and he is thus in a state of flow.

A radical enlivening of self is needed to transform us from a condition of Tumah and blockage, to a condition of Tehara and flow. What makes a Mikvah such a portal into the experience of renewal?

Mikvah is spelled מקוה, which can also be read as *mi-Kaveh /* from קוה, 'from hope'. In the Torah the word *Mikvah* is also used to mean 'hope'. The Prophet Yirmiyahu [*Jeremiah*, 14:8] praises the Source of Life: *Mikveh Yisrael Moshi'o b'Eis Tzarah /* "O Hope of Israel, his Savior at a time of trouble...." A Mikvah is thus a place of *Tikvah /* hope. When we enter a Mikvah we are being birthed again into a place of yearning, hoping and dreaming. We are reclaiming our Neshamah, our soul, our Infinity, linked forever with the Infinite power of the *Ohr Ein Sof /* Infinite Light of the Creator. Immersion in the Mikvah is an *Aschalta /* beginning, an opening, into a state of wholesomeness and Tikkun. We must of course then take the necessary steps and walk through that opening to continue the process of purification and rectification begun in the Mikvah.

Ultimately, what gives rise to anger is a type of rigidity, a stuck Tumah-influenced way of thinking and interacting with life. The root of this rigid way of knowing and expecting is *Yeshus* / ego. When Yeshus dominates a person's perception, it causes him to think that he knows how life ought to be and how events should unfold. Whenever we hold too tightly onto an image of ourself, or fasten our imagination on what we think is to be expected, and the facts on the ground do not seem to match up, we think our whole life is being disrupted and we become angry. This 'narrative of anger' grabs our attention when we have constructed in our minds how people should rightfully act toward us. How could so-and-so say that to *me*? How can this happen to *me*? All these are statements of Yeshus, the egoic 'me' in distress over a perception of life veering off course.

If you are driving carefully down the highway and a car comes out of nowhere and cuts you off, perhaps you will become agitated and angry: *'I' am driving responsibly, and 'they' are driving recklessly. 'They' deserve to be reprimanded and punished, and 'I' am the one to do it.* When we identify as Yeshus, we reactively separate ourselves from the other and seek to blame and punish them, because our fragile ego lives in perpetual fear of being blamed, punished and disrupted. To gain a sense of inviolability, we construct a *Kelipah* / shell of rigid self-righteousness around ourselves.

When we make ourselves rigid and unyielding, we constantly get hurt. The slightest disappointment or unfavorable glance jostles us, because we have no inner cushioning. Everything is taken as personal and deliberately directed at us. We become stuck in wanting to know, 'Why me'? But we are unfortunately blinded to the implicit answer to this question: 'Why?' '...Me!' — my increased suffering is because of the sense of 'me', the sense of Yeshus that I have created and hardened around my true self.

Immersing in Ayin & the Name E'he'yeh:

Our *Ani* / 'I' or Yeshus can seem to be what we really are. To undo this spiritual Tum'ah caused by fixed identification, we need to enter into a state of *Ayin* / emptiness of form. From there we can emerge fresh into a new healthy, Tahor *Ani* / 'I'. This authentic, essential 'I' includes both the Yeshus of the body and the Ayin of the transcendent soul, transcending and including both sides of the existential dichotomy within a radically inclusive unity.

To release the false, irritable Ani for the real, grounded Ani, the essence of who we really are, we need to go through a process in which we temporarily shed all self-images. In this intermediary stage, the lower image is no longer, but neither have we regained the higher image. In order to transform one form into another there is always a transitional stage where it is neither this nor that. If you wish to make a table into a chair you need to first deconstruct the table, and then you can use the pieces of wood to construct the chair. There has to be a moment when we let go of the old, and allow the table to cease being what it was. Likewise, we need to first surrender and deconstruct the lower Ani. We need to let ourselves be 'nothing' for a few moments, immersed in Ayin, before resurfacing into the newness of our authentic Ani.

When we immerse in the Mikvah, we are meditatively immersing in Ayin-consciousness. To maximize the effectiveness of this practice, we should place our entire Kavanah on the Name *E'he'yeh*

/ I Will Be. We should try to actually visualize the letters of this sacred Name and contemplate what it means. Here are is some background for this Kavanah:

Mikvah, in numerical value, is 151, which is the same value as the *Milu'i* / fullness of the Name *E'he'yeh* / I Will Be, the Divine Name revealed to Moshe at the burning bush [*Sha'ar HaKavanos*, Erev Shabbos]. In other words, there are four letters in the Name Ehe-yeh: Aleph, Hei, Yud, Hei. When these letters are themselves spelled out, their total numerical value is 151.

Aleph is spelled: Aleph/1, Lamed/30, Pei/80. This equals 111.

Hei is spelled: Hei/5, Hei/5. This equals 10.

Yud is spelled: Yud/10, Vav/6. Dalet/4. This equals 20.

Hei is spelled: Hei/5, Hei/5. This equals 10

111 + 10 + 20 + 10 = 151*

*Another way to reach 151 is to square each of the letters of *E'he'yeh* and then add them together: Aleph is 1, and 1 x 1 = 1. Hei is 5, and 5 x 5 = 25. (1+25=26). Yud is 10, and 10 x 10 = 100 (1+25+100=126). Hei is 5, and 5 x 5 = 25. 1 + 25 + 100 + 25 = 151 [*Sha'ar haPesukim*, Pinchas].

The Name *E'he'yeh* is related to the future and 'becoming'. *E'he'yeh Asher E'he'yeh*, is translated by some people as "I Am That I Am," but more accurately, it means, 'I Will Be That Which I *Will* Be.' This means 'I will be with them now, and I will be with them in their future as well' [*Rashi*, Shemos, 3:14]. 'I, Who am expressed through everything in the present moment of Being, am also expressed through the future, as *Becoming*.'

When we enter the Mikvah, the fluid body of living water we can have Kavanah on the Name *E'he'yeh*, the Divine *Ko'ach* / power that engenders movement, liberation and becoming. In this way we become en-souled again, and we become alive as our Chayus returns to our bodies and minds. We become free from being stuck in the past. Now we can feel refreshed, purified of the pollution of anger and negative attachments. Now we have hope in the possibilities of the future. We vividly and viscerally feel more joyful and free.

Practice:

The next time you flare up in anger at others, or even at yourself or the world around you, take your first opportunity to go to a Mikvah. To undo our energetic contractions and narrow patterns of thinking we need to immerse ourselves in 'water'—a fluid, transient, undefined reality. We need to enter *Ayin* so that we can re-emerge as a new, living, breathing, integrated *Ani* / I.

When you are removing your garments before immersing, do so with the Kavanah of taking off layers of Kelipah, shedding the rigid shells of assumptions and expectations. Sense how you are already a little lighter and more free, even before actual immersion. When you enter into the sacred waters of the Mikvah, feel the water surrounding your body and mind, and sense that you are on the threshold of *Olam haBa* / the 'Becoming World', the realm of purity, pure potential and integrated Ayin-consciousness. Then, as you are immersing, contemplate the Name *E'he'yeh* as the Divine Koach that gives you future life, possibility, fluidity, freshness and hope. Under the water, feel any remaining chaos of anger dissolving away forever, and when you break the surface sense how your soul has fully returned to you. As you ascend from the waters, feel the Koach of having been revived, renewed, strengthened, and rededicated to engage in life from the place of health, balance, rectification and wholesomeness.

☾

SUMMARY OF TEVES

*I*N THE MONTH OF TEVES, THE EXTREME COLD OF THE SEASON stimulates us to seek warmth with other people. Indeed, one of the meanings of the **name** of the month is 'good for intimacy'. In order to truly get closer to others in a meaningful way, however, we need to ameliorate our addiction to chaotic emotions such as anger, which is the **sense** of the month. *Gedi* / goat, the **sign** of the month, represents this self-destructively impulsive and self-centeredly possessive energy, which is characterized by Eisav. The tendency to objectify, instrumentalize, manipulate and abuse others for our own purposes others is precisely what we need to confront during this time.

The **letter sequence of Hashem's name** indicates that there are very few revealed blessings flowing into the world during this month, implying that we must therefore redouble our efforts to elevate ourselves. The **Torah portions** read in this month detail the Exile in Egypt, and are full of harsh spiritual contraction. Yet, they also also teach us how to be present with and move beyond the egoic harshness within ourselves.

The three letters of the word Teves form an acronym and reveal a deeper dimension of this month: *Tov B'reishis Tohu* / 'goodness within the head (or source) of chaos'. This is the path of sweetening the month's energetic harshness by finding the hidden goodness within its source or 'beginning'. *Kaved* / liver is the **body part** of the month. *Kaved* also means 'heavy', alluding to the emotional baggage that we carry around with us when we become trapped within our own self-fulfilling narratives. The stories in our heads that we use to justify our responses to the sensations we experience are a source of egoic negativity.

One of the skills of the **tribe** Dan is 'to gather in what is dropped'. Our human tendency is to 'drop' certain intense energies and sensations when they are uncomfortable, by forcefully suppressing them or unconsciously acting out in response. However, Dan teaches us that we can gather in and include our raw sensations. When we disengage from our heavy narratives that weigh us down and stay present with sensory experience as it arises, even our sensations of anger can be 'gathered' and integrated within us in such a way that they are converted into fuel for positive and productive action.

The **letter** of the month is Ayin, which means 'eye', alluding to our tendency to perceive only the immediate surface of things. When we are fully present with our experience, our eyes will be open to recognize the Divine Presence hiding in our lives, even within seeming negativity.

The Fast of the Tenth of Teves (the '**holiday**' of the month) is called the 'beginning of the hardship', referring to the beginning of the destruction of the Temple and the subsequent exile. When we fast on this day, we have a heightened opportunity to meet the source of chaos and negativity head-on and gather in its hidden goodness.

To "exalt" or praise, as expressed in the **verse** of the month, is the opposite of anger, chaos and possessiveness. Praising completes our Tikkun and sweetening of the egoism, brute physicality and negativity in our relationships. When we make this Tikkun, this month will be truly "good for intimacy", both human and Divine. The coldness and dryness of the **element** of earth both expresses the harshness and physicality of Teves, and also hints at our potential intimacy with the 'unmovable' Ground of Being, the Divine Essence.

THE 12 DIMENSIONS OF TEVES	
SEQUENCE OF HASHEM'S NAME	Hei-Yud-Hei-Vav
TORAH VERSE	"Hashem is with me and thus I exalt His Name…."
LETTER	Ayin *(meaning 'eye')*
MONTH NAME	**Teves** is an acronym for **Tov B'Reishis Tohu** / 'Goodness within the head or source of Tohu'
SENSE	**Rogez** / anger
SIGN OF THE ZODIAC	**Gedi** / the goat (Capricorn); chaotic energy
TRIBE	**Dan**; the gatherers of what was dropped, the rear-garde
BODY PART	**Kaved** / liver
ELEMENT	**Earth** (cold & dry)
PARSHIOS / TORAH PORTIONS	Narrative of the Egyptian Exile
SEASON	Deep winter
HOLIDAY	Fast of the Tenth of Teves

APPENDIX A:
Five Levels of Relationship

Love is a verb, an active state of being, of simultaneously giving and receiving. It is impossible to 'have' love as an object. Certainly, we cannot 'have' a person, or possess them like an object. We can only be love and offer love.

In all relationships there are various levels of presence and connection with the other. There is also an important distinction between the 'who' and the 'what.' In your relationships, you should carefully inspect this matter. Do you love, understand or respect the 'who', the person him or herself — or merely the 'what', what they do, how they look, think, experience or express themselves?

Even close relationships often begin with a predominant awareness of the 'what' of the other person. But for any maturity and true closeness to form, you need to grow into a predominant awareness of the true 'who' of the beloved. If not, then when the 'what' changes, such as any shift in outward beauty, wealth, power, fame or viewpoint — or if you change, such as if your interest in those specific appearances or accomplishments turns to boredom — the relationship itself will end. It will become painfully clear that there never was an authentic relationship at all. The so-called relationship was just a projection of selfish desires or utilitarian self-interests.

Our Sages teach [*Ta'anis* 24a], "Regarding a (potential) bride who (still) lives in the house of her father: so long as her eyes are (seen as) beautiful, her body needs no examination." What does this mean? Eyes are the only feature of the body that do not appear to age. When you get older, and you see a reflection or a photo of your face, sometimes your eyes are the only part that you can recognize as yours. Every other part changes in shape and tone. After a few decades of being apart, others may look at you for some time before they focus on your eyes and suddenly recognize you.

Romantics say that "the eyes are the windows to the soul," but our Sages take this to an even deeper level. If we fall in love with a person's 'eyes', meaning their unchanging soul, we can be sure that our love will be real and lasting, and that we will always love them for 'who' they are, not just for 'what' they do for us. The 'who' is the unchanging essence of a person.

This is the way of viewing and relating to people that can undo the 'seeing of *Tohu*' / chaos, which is the 'seeing of Eisav'. The twin brother of Yaakov, Eisav, sees nothing deeper than the surface, the bodily appearance and the immediate, temporary aspects of things. He sees only what might gratify him or threaten him, in that moment.

Teves is a time when the body comes into focus. However, on the ultimate level, the body is an expression of the essential 'who', the *Yesh Amiti* / True Existence, the Essence of Reality. The word *Guf* / body, can also mean 'self'. As the Tzemach Tzedek writes, souls are produced Davka / specifically when a Guf comes together with a Guf, without any intervening garments. So too, in our relationship with Hashem, the greatest productivity and soulfulness is born when we meet self-to-Self, essence-to-Essence, eye-to-Eye, with nothing intervening.

Five Levels of Relationship

There are five levels of human relationship corresponding to five broad stages of development, the Five Worlds, the Five Levels of the Soul, and five levels of relationship with the Divine. These levels are 'i' (ego), 'i-it', 'i-you', 'no-i', and 'I-I'.

i — The first level is the lone 'i' of ego, which is actually closed off to any real relationship. Here there is no 'other', because a sense of self-interest blocks all else. This is also the base 'physical self' which dominates and propels our consciousness in infancy. For an infant, others are not truly experienced. A parent is a mere extension of oneself; 'When I cry, I am fed, I am cleaned, or I am held.' Sadly, under certain conditions, adults can stagnate at this level as well. This lack of a possibility for relationship corresponds to the

World of Asiyah. In this dense, physical world, one can somehow feel and posit that the Source of Life does not exist, and even that 'i' am the source or the center of it all.

i-it — In this level, 'others' begin to exist, however they are perceived as objects which may be useful or detrimental to the perceived needs and narrative of the self. The needs and feelings of the other don't yet exist. There may be an emotional attachment to another, but it is still in the self-oriented mode of a child. For example, a child is aware of the existence of 'mother' and 'father', but innocently feels they only exist in order to provide food, shelter, toys and affection. Adults, too, often objectify and use each other. This level corresponds to the World of Yetzirah, the realm of emotion. In this stage of consciousness, one might realize their own neediness and pray with emotion, but the Divine is still seen to be an 'it', a separate or distant 'object' of some kind.

i-You — In this level, one becomes aware that others exist as real people. One appreciates that people have their own personalities, feelings, desires and needs. This is the beginning of authentic, mutual relationship, and of truly understanding someone else. When children mature or perhaps reach adulthood, they can develop a capacity for authentic relationship with their parents and community. This corresponds to the World of Beriyah, the realm of 'understanding'. In this stage of consciousness, one actually appreciates the presence of the Creator. Prayer and study become real dialogues, with a vivid sense of mutual understanding.

No i — In this level of relationship there is a certain kind of absence or emptiness of self. For example, when mature persons fall deeply in love with one another, they can lose their separate, distinct 'i'. Effectively, in this state there remain no personal desires; everything is fully dedicated to- and overwhelmed by the other. This corresponds to the World of Atzilus, the transcendent realm of 'overwhelming closeness' and absorption. In this stage of consciousness, one is in total *Bitul* / self-nullification in the presence of the Infinite One. There are no personal needs and no separate person praying, just timeless silence, stillness, and Light.

I-I — In this fifth and consummate level of maturity in relationship, the essential 'true self' of both subjects is fully recognized and regarded. Both are paradoxically aware of being a 'oneness' and yet 'two individuals' at the same time. This is truly 'seeing eye-to-eye', as there is really only one eye, one awareness, seeing through both pairs of eyes. It is truly being 'I-to-I', as there is one 'I' being through both beings.

This corresponds to the World of Adam Kadmon, or *Atzmus* / Essence and Moshe is the prime example of this reality. In *Devarim* / Deuteronomy, the fifth book of the Torah, he is emerges fully as an individual person, yet at the same time, his essence is none other than the Divine Essence. It is Moshe who is speaking in this Book, and yet he says, "...And *I* will give you rain." Through the Torah of Moshe, we too can reach this level, especially when we "make our will the Divine will." We do this when we are performing the *Mitzvos* / Divine actions in this world, and we are, at that moment, *Panim el Panim* / face-to-Face, or body-to-Body, with Hashem. I exist independently, and yet my will is Hashem's will. I am speaking, and yet my words are words of Divine Torah. I am praising, and yet my praises are *Tehilasecha* / Your praises.

In the Month of Teves we have a special opportunity to touch this world of Essence, as it is *Yerech sheNeheneh Guf min haGuf* / "a month in which 'self' takes pleasure from 'Self'" [*Megilah*, 13a]. We have an opportunity to tap into this fifth level of relationship, both with people and with Hashem.

One way to access the highest level of human relationship is as the Gemara teaches: "Someone who prays for another, *v'Hu Tzarich l'Oso Davar* / and he needs the same thing, he will be answered first" [*Bava Kama*, 92a]. What happens, however, if the person who is praying does not "need the same thing"? Here is a *Chassidishe Peshat* / a Chasidic explanation: the person should pray for the other *as if* he needs the same thing. When you pray for someone, sense how the other person is not separate from you; his loss is ultimately 'your loss' and his need is ultimately your need. When you are so open that you feel the other person's pain or lack, you can pray from such love and oneness of identity, that your prayers for yourself are answered simultaneously, or even "first".

A couple can realize the highest levels in their relationship when both people independently realize that it is not romance or 'gazing into each other's eyes' that counts the most. It is gazing in the same direction, seeing from within the same unchanging 'I'. During this month, focus on all your relationships until you can find the deeper unity, the single essential identity, between yourself and others.

☾

Summary

i	Self-absorption	Asiyah, body
i-it	Self-separation, utilitarianism	Yetzirah, emotion
i-You	Connection, understanding the other	Beriah, intellect
No i	Absorption in the other, self-transcendence	Atzilus, infinite closeness
I-I	'Inclusive transcendence' or relationship of others within one essence	Adam Kadmon / 'Primordial' or ultimate human-Divine identity

APPENDIX B:
The Tenth of Teves: The Beginning (and End) of All Exiles

THE TENTH OF TEVES IS THE DAY THE BABYLONIAN EMPEROR, Nevuchadnetzar / Nebuchadnezzar, began his siege on Yerushalayim / Jerusalem. Thirty months later, in Tamuz, the city walls were breached, and on the Ninth of Av of that year the First Beis haMikdash was finally set aflame.

As explored earlier, the Tenth of Teves is a very serious fast day, so much so, that it apparently has the power to push aside Shabbos: if the Tenth of Teves would theoretically be on Shabbos, we would fast rather than feast on that Shabbos. Compare this to the very stringent fast of the Ninth of Av, which is postponed to the following day when it falls out on Shabbos.

The question that arises is threefold: a) why is the fast of the Tenth of Teves so serious? b) in fact, why is it a fast day at all? and c) more pointedly, why is the related ancient history relevant to us?

The reason for commemorating fast days which correspond to events in our collective history is that we are all still living with the effects of those events. In the words of the Rambam, "There are days when the entire Jewish people fast because of the calamities that occurred to them then, to arouse hearts and initiate the paths of Teshuvah. This (fasting) will serve as a reminder of *our* deviant conduct, and that of our ancestors which resembles our present conduct, and therefore (we will be reminded that the same conduct is what) brought these calamities upon them and upon *us*" [*Hilchos Ta'anis*, 5:1].

With this in mind, it makes perfect sense to fast for the destruction of the Beis haMikdash on the Ninth of Av, since on that day we are living in the effect and in the same reality — living without a Beis haMikdash. *We* mourn because "the calamities (were brought) upon them and upon *us*." But why fast on the Tenth of Teves as well? In the words of the Rambam: "The Tenth of Teves: this is the day...the King of Babylon camped against Jerusalem and placed the city under siege" [ibid, 2]. Why is it relevant when the siege began, and how does that impact *us*?

At the end of the Gemara in Ta'anis, which speaks about the laws of fasting, our sages discuss the fast of the Ninth of Av. Rabbi Yochanan says, "If I was in that generation (of the destruction) I would have established the fast day on the *Tenth of Av*, since most of the (First) Beis haMikdash was burned down on the Tenth of

Av. Why, then, asks the Gemara, did the sages establish the fast on the Ninth of Av? Because the Ninth is the *Aschalta d'Puranusa* / the beginning of that particular event of devastation and hardship [*Ta'anis*, 29a].

Thus ensues a debate: does the beginning of a tragedy or the culmination of a tragedy demand mourning? The decision of the Gemara implies that — for the most part — we fast and mourn on the *Aschalta* / the beginning of a given tragedy.

This same logic applies to the Tenth of Teves [*Bnei Yissachar*, Kislev/Teves, Ma'amar 14:1]. This is the day the Babylonian Emperor Nevuchadnetzar began to lay siege on Jerusalem. Thirty months later, in the month of Tamuz, the city walls were breached. On the Ninth Av of that same year, the First Beis haMikdash was rent asunder. Thus the eventual destruction of the Beis haMikdash, and the subsequent exile from the Land of Israel, began on the Tenth of Teves. The Tenth of Teves is therefore the *original* Aschalta d'Puranusa [*Likutei Sichos*, 15:421]which culminated on the Ninth and Tenth of Av.

This helps to explain, perhaps, why the fast is so serious even today: it is the beginning of the destruction and exile that we are all still experiencing here and now. On the other hand, if we are currently living in the effects of the *Churban* / destruction, why do we care so much about the day it all began so many hundreds, even thousands, of years ago?

The Opening of the Possibility of Exile

On a deeper level, *Aschalta d'Puranusa* means not only the historical date of the beginning of the destruction, but the archetypal 'opening of the possibility' for exile, hardship and destruction. This possibility is present within our life, no matter the place, time or situation we are living in. In an unredeemed reality there is always the possibility that whatever measure of peace and security that we have, and whatever utilitarian or emotional connection to the Divine we have, could change for the worse.

In the course of Jewish history, we were in exile and enslaved in Egypt, and then Hashem took us out of Egypt and brought us to Mount Sinai. With Matan Torah we were totally freed of our past enslavement and oppression, and free to choose a new life full of Torah and meaning. We were transformed into an existentially liberated people, a *Ben Chorin* / child of freedom.

Then, Hashem gave us the Mishkan, the portable Mikdash [*Eiruvin*, 2a] in the Desert. When we entered the promised Land of Israel, the Mishkan entered with us and was established in Israel. At some points in time, it remained for hundreds of years in a single location. Then, King David received instructions to start gathering the materials for his son, King Shlomo to build the Beis haMikdash in a permanent location in the holy city of Yerushalayim.

It appeared that this would be the linear trajectory of Klal Yisrael: living with a permanent Beis haMikdash in our homeland until the arrival and revelation of Moshiach. But then a drastic event occurred, disrupting everything. An invading army managed to lay siege on Yerushalayim. All of a sudden, the relative peace and security of living in the Land of Israel with the Beis haMikdash was shattered. The possibility became real that the course of Jewish history might unfold in a much different way; the Beis haMikdash might be destroyed, and we might no longer live in our homeland among prophets and the revealed presence of the Shechinah.

Before this siege, who could have imagined life *without* a central physical place to intimately connect with Hashem, a place where one could come and immediately see the Divine Presence? [*Chagigah*, 2b]. Who could have imagined being dispersed to the four corners of the world and enduring thousands of years of hardship?

This is the deeper reason that we mourn and fast on the Tenth of Teves, the Aschalta d'Puranusa. It is the timeless moment in which the very possibility of destruction and exile becomes a reality. Not only did this impact our ancestors, but it impacts us as well, both collectively and personally. By fasting, we sensitize ourselves to suffering, and we mourn all manifestations of tragedy and alienation, whether external or internal, physical, emotional, mental or spiritual.

The Four Externally Imposed Exiles & the Internal Exile

There are four grand, externally-imposed exiles that Klal Yisrael experienced: the Babylonian, Persian, Greek and Roman exiles. In addition, there is an internal exile related to the dissension within

Klal Yisrael, the breaking apart of the unity of Klal Yisrael. This began with the emergence of theological factions which eroded the harmony within Klal Yisrael during the time of the Second Beis haMikdash.

When the Babylonian army conquered and destroyed the First Holy Temple, Klal Yisrael was exiled mostly to Babylon. When the Persian Empire conquered the Babylonians, the Jews in Babylon began living under Persian rule. It was during this reign that Haman was inspired to rise up and destroy the Jewish People, giving rise to the story and holiday of Purim.

After 70 years of exile, the Persian Emperor gave permission for Klal Yisrael to resettle in the Land of Israel and rebuild the Beis haMikdash. Principal among the leaders of Klal Yisrael at that time was Ezra *haSofer* / the Scribe.

Under the guidance of Ezra the Scribe many Jews, but not all, returned to Yerushalayim and built the Second Beis haMikdash. A few hundred years into the Second Temple period a new threat arose. Alexander the Great was capturing and conquering most of the known world. His rule soon enveloped the entire area of ancient Israel. Desiring to unify his entire empire, he devised to establish a universal culture, establishing Alexandria as its center in Egypt, and populating that city with people from across the globe. His idea of universal culture was a blend of Greek theology and philosophy called Hellenism, with some added elements of Eastern thought. Sadly, among the Jews living in Israel there were those who embraced Greek culture, and became known as *Misyavanim* / Hellenizers.

Following the death of Alexander the Great, his empire fractured and was divided between some of his generals. Ptolemy the First took control over Egypt while Seleucus the First began the Seleucid Dynasty and took control over Syria. The Land of Israel, in the middle, went back and forth between the control of these two Greek powers.

The Chanukah story happened during this period. This story was the effect of a deeper struggle between our Torah values and ideals, and the inauthentic 'exile' ideals of the imposing Greek power. The Greeks were not interested in killing Jewish bodies [*Levush*, *Bach* and *Taz* on Orach Chayim, 670. Ma'amor *Mai Chanukah*, 5701] or even their spirits, but rather in enfolding them within the universalist Greek Empire by indoctrinating them with Hellenism and toppling their authentically Jewish intellectual and spiritual worldview.

The Second Beis haMikdash was finally destroyed by the Romans. The Roman Empire, with her offspring, Western civilization, has inflicted near-constant pressure on the Jewish People, beginning with the expulsion of all Jews from Israel at the time of the destruction. This oppression continued through many massacres, pogroms and holocausts, and continues even today through anti-semitic propaganda, the pressure of assimilation and the enticement of secularism. Ever since the destruction of the Second Beis haMikdash there has been one continuous battle on all fronts between the spirit of 'Rome' and the spirit of 'Jerusalem'.

These are all the external 'enemies' of Klal Yisrael, yet, there is also an internal exile of factionalization and dissension within Klal Yisrael. During the Second Beis haMikdash period, besides the external, existential threats of the Greeks and Romans, there began a deeper erosion within the *K'lal* / the collective soul of the Jewish people. Even 500 years after the destruction, the situation was so perilous that the Sages inserted an additional passage into the Amidah prayer [See *Berachos*, 28b] to counter the internal threat of certain factions.

This added passage, which today starts with the word *ve-Lamalshinim* / "And the informers..," referred to Jews who would inform the Roman authorities against their brethren. In some other versions, and in certain periods of time, the first word of this insertion was *Meshumadim* / those who denounce Torah and Mitzvos, or *Tzedukim* / the Sadducees, or *Minim* / heretics, or *Notzrim* / Nazoreans, those who followed a man claimed by his students to be Moshiach. These are all factions that originally began *within* Klal Yisrael and caused great division and hardship, and terrible persecution of the faithful Jews under their rule.

What happened on the Three Harsh Days of Teves?

In the *Selichos* / special prayers for forgiveness that we recite on the fast of the Tenth of Teves, it says, regarding "...three afflictions during this month of Teves: I instituted a fast on the Eighth, Ninth and Tenth of Teves." What are these three events? On the Eighth of Teves we were forced to translate the Torah: "The Greek King forced me to write the Torah in Greek." As recorded in the Shulchan Aruch [*Orach Chayim*, 580:1], "On the Eighth of Teves the Torah was written (translated) into Greek (called the *Septuagint*) in the days of Talmi (Ptolemy the Second) the King, and darkness descended to the world for three days." [See the end of *Megilas Ta'anis*.] On the Tenth of Teves, as we know, the King of Babylon camped against Yerushalayim and placed the city under siege. What happened on the Ninth? This text does not say clearly. As the Shulchan Aruch comments, "(Regarding) the Ninth, it is not known who caused the trouble that happened on it."

We learn from other sources, including the Ashkenaz version of Selichos, that on the Ninth of Teves, in the year 3448 (313 BCE), Ezra the Scribe passed away. [The Sefardic Selichos, however, says that he passed away on the Tenth of Teves.] Ezra was born in Babylon, and was a scribe of Torah scrolls by profession. He later led a group of thousands of Jews from Babylon to resettle the homeland of Israel, and became their spiritual leader. Indeed, his death would have been seen by some as a very harsh event.

Some older sources write that the Ninth of Teves is the birthday of the founder of *Natzrus*. Obviously, both that and the death of Ezra could be true. The present point is, however, that the four events mentioned — the translation of the Torah into Greek, the death of Ezra, the birth of the founder of Natzrus, and the siege of Yerushalayim — each correspond to one of our four externally-imposed exiles. And even if, in the time they occurred, these four events were not in themselves catastrophic, they were expressions of the *Aschalta d'Puranusa*. They paved the way for the effects of the four external exiles to take hold, making space for the fifth, internal exile to splinter Klal Yisrael into factions, for the all-important unity of the People to erode even until our times.

Tenth of Teves: The Babylonian & Persian Exiles

On the Tenth of Teves, when the holy city of Yerushalayim was besieged, it opened up the possibility that later the emperor Nevuchadnetzar would be able to breach the city walls and eventually set the First Beis haMikdash ablaze. The siege therefore led directly to the Babylonian exile, as once the Beis haMikdash was destroyed, the Jews were forced to move to the land of Babylon.

A short time later, as mentioned previously, the Persian Empire overthrew the Babylonian Kingdom. The Jewish people living in Babylon found themselves subjects of the Persian Empire, which led seamlessly into the story of Purim. Haman came in front of the king of Persia and said, "There is a nation who is dispersed among the nations, but whose faith is different." The dispersion he mentioned was of course due to the Babylonian Exile, which had become the Persian Exile. Thus the event of the Tenth of Teves led directly to two of our four external exiles. An allusion to the Persian Exile's connection with Teves is found in Megillas Ester when it says the king of Persia took Esther as a wife "in the month of Teves".

The Eighth of Teves:
Translation of the Torah & the Greek Exile

"On the Eighth of Teves, the Torah was translated into Greek and a darkness descended to the world for three days." Elsewhere we learn, "Seventy sages translated the Torah into Greek for King Ptolemy. That day was as difficult for the people of Israel as the day on which the Golden Calf was fashioned, for the Torah could not be fully translated." [Small Tractates, *Soferim* 1:7, *Sefer Torah*, 1:8.]

On the other hand, the Torah tells us, "On the other side of the Jordan, in the land of Moav, Moshe began to explain the Torah, saying…" [*Devarim*, 1:5]. As Rashi notes, Moshe then explained the Torah in 70 languages, one for each of the 'Seventy Nations' of the world. From this it would seem that the translation of the Torah is not such a horrific event, rather it could be a part of the whole project of Matan Torah: the wisdom of the Torah was meant to reach the far corners of the world and permeate all languages.

Furthermore, following the passage in Gemara [*Megilah*, 9a] which describes the translation of the Torah into Greek by 70 different Sages, it says that Hashem placed wisdom into the heart of each and every one (of the 70 translators), and they had one common understanding. That is, each translation, although made independently, turned out to be identical. This could only have been accomplished through *Ruach haKodesh* / Divine spirit. The Gemara continues, "Rabban Shimon ben Gamliel says: Even with regard to Torah scrolls, the Sages permitted them to be written (translated) only in Greek…. (And) the law is in accordance with the opinion of Rabban Shimon ben Gamliel. Rabbi Yochanan said: What is the reason for the opinion of Rabban Shimon ben Gamliel? He based his opinion on an allusion in the Torah, as the verse states: "Hashem shall enlarge Yefes (alluding to Yavan a descendent of Yefes, the forbear of the Greeks) and He shall dwell in the tents of Shem (alluding to Klal Yisrael, Shem's descendants)" [*Bereishis*, 9:27]. *Yefes* is etymologically similar to the Hebrew term for beauty, *Yofi*, as in, "The beauty of Yefes shall be in the tents of Shem."

This means that theoretically, a person could write a Sefer Torah, the most sacred object we have, in Greek, and it would be just as valid as one that is written in *Ashuri* / Hebrew. [Although this is no longer relevant, since the pure Greek language has been lost; Rambam, *Hilchos Tefilin*, 1:19.]

Perhaps the ruling of Shimon ben Gamliel implies that since it was already properly translated by the sages into Greek, and since the language was familiar among the Sages, therefore it could be written in Greek [Rambam, *Pirush haMishnayos*, Megilah, 2:1]. Either way, our Sages tell us that there is beauty in the tents of Klal Yisrael when the Torah has been translated into the beautiful Greek language.

All of this further compounds our quandary. Is translation of the Torah positive and beautiful, or is it "as bad as the day of the making of the Golden Calf"? To understand this more deeply, we need to read carefully the words of the Sages' seeming negative remark. They do not say that translating the Torah is difficult like the day that Klal Yisrael served and worshipped the Golden Calf, rather, "like the day the Golden Calf was *fashioned*" — which was the day before it was worshipped.

Moshe had ascended the mountain, and was late in his return, in the estimation of the People. The masses came before Aharon and said, "Arise, fashion for us an *Elokim* (god or powerful leader) that shall walk before us, for the man Moshe, who brought us up out of the Land of Egypt — we do not know what has become of him" [*Shemos*, 32:1].

The day the Golden Calf was fashioned was *potentially* negative, but not essentially. What they asked for was just an image or conduit that would replace the powerful presence of Moshe. They did not state that they wanted to worship an idol, rather a medium through which to connect to the Transcendence of Hashem, an object that would function like a Moshe. Yet, on the *next* day, they looked at that object and declared, 'This is god,' and did in fact worship it.

The problem with translating the Torah is thus not in the actual translation itself. The proof of this is, even Moshe translated it into 70 languages. Rather, the problem is what translation and accessibility of the Torah can lead to when its readers are not guided and possessing humility. The problem is what could happen the 'next day'[*Likutei Sichos* 24:3-4].

Once the Torah was translated, there was an illusion that one no longer needed a *Mesorah* / living tradition, or the guidance of a living teacher. It appeared as though anyone could pick up a translation of the Torah and fully understand it. This led to the possibility and the opening of the Greek exile, the threat of Hellenism and its worship of intellect alone. True, the Torah is a 'book of wisdom', but it is a Divine Wisdom, a living path that connects us to the Infinite Transcendent One. The Written Torah is inseparable from the Oral Torah, the revealed interpretation, guidance, and practice of Torah. But the Greeks and the Hellenized Jews saw Torah as a mere text, not as a perpetual dialogue with the Divine. They argued: 'You may study the Torah, and even do so diligently, but do it as with any other wisdom teaching of the world.' They attempted to replace the oral, integral, dialogic, spiritual path of Torah with an intellectual, individual, literary perspective on Torah. This popular 'replacement theology' was the real exile of the Greeks.

The Greeks desired to make Klal Yisrael forget that it is Hashem's Torah, as we say in the prayers on Chanukah: the Greeks wished to "make them forget *Torasecha* / Your Torah." Their whole belittling rendition of Torah as a human philosophy was made possible by the translation of the Torah into their language. Their very ability to make the argument came from their un-guided and free access to the text.

Ultimately, the process that Moshe initiated with his own translations will be complete, and the Torah will be revealed within all the languages of the world. This will be the full Torah of Hashem, flowing like purest water through all the languages of the world, without it becoming trapped and stagnate in the *Kelipah* of human words, intellect or prejudice. At which point we will be able to perceive the clear light of Hashem communicated within each and every possible vessel, no matter its color or contour.

Ninth of Teves: Birth of the founder of Natzrus & the Roman Exile

When Rome accepted Natzrus as the religion of the Empire, it became the embodiment of Natzrus, along with the chaos and harsh exile that Natzrus has inflicted on the Jewish People throughout many thousands of years.

However, the birth of the leader of Natzrus was in itself only *potentially* negative. It was merely the birth of another Jewish child. Even when he grew older, it was not inevitable that his followers would create a widespread movement of hatred, massacre, torture, crusades and pogroms — but they did. All of these great hardships that Klal Yisrael suffered were an outcome of his birth, this *Aschalta d'Puranusa*. The exile of Klal Yisrael by Rome and the Western 'civilized' world was conceived with the birth of this religion and its founder.

Ninth of Teves:
Death of Ezra the Scribe & the Internal Exile

Perhaps the greatest threat to Klal Yisrael comes from within the community itself. The death of Ezra is linked with the birth of the founder of Natzrus and the basic ideas of Natzrus, which are both expressions of the greater exile that began in that time.

To review: Ezra, the great prophet and leader of Klal Yisrael, 'gathered' the nation from within the Babylonian Exile, and helped them return to their Homeland. He assisted in building the Second Beis haMikdash, the central place to connect with Hashem. Some years after he passed on, during the latter period of the Second Beis haMikdash, came the birth and rise of the founder of Natzrus. This new and divisive movement caused tremendous hardship, friction, and fraction within Klal Yisrael. Later, when Natzrus made a substantial break from Klal Yisrael, its followers became some of the worst persecutors (Heaven forbid) of Klal Yisrael in all of history.

Ezra, together with his contemporaries, Chagai, Zecharya, and Malachi (who Rabbi Yehudah says is Ezra himself, *Megilah,* 15a), was of the last of the Prophets. Ezra and his colleagues initiated the era of the Second Beis haMikdash. When they all passed away and left the world, so did *Ruach haKodesh* / Divine Spirit of prophecy [*Sotah*, 48b. *Sanhedrin*, 88b]. Ezra himself is so identified with Ruach haKodesh and the resting of the Shechinah in this world, that our Sages declare that if someone is worthy for the Shechinah to rest upon them as it rested upon Moshe (e.g. Hillel the elder), this person is considered a student of Ezra [*Sanhedrin*, 11a].

When Ezra and his contemporaries passed and the classical age of prophecy came to a close, the body of Torah, Prophets and Writings was sealed and canonized. The era in which Hashem spoke to us and we simply listened and received, ended. Ezra is not called a 'rabbi', but rather a *Sofer* / Scribe, as in one who 'transcribes' words that are received from Above. Why did the era of *Torah shel-Baal Peh* / the oral revelation of Torah, the age of the rabbis, need to begin in this period? Having been saturated and imbued with revelation from Above, it came time for us to start to 'do the talking', as it were, in the mode of 'revelation from below'.

At the close of the paradigm of 'revelation from Above' and prophecy, the era of revealed miracles also came to a close. The miracles that were present in the First Beis haMikdash were not revealed during the Second Beis haMikdash [*Yumah*, 21b], however many miracles did manifest there. Shimon *haTzadik* / Simon the Righteous was the primary student of Ezra, as the Rambam writes [Hakdamah, *Mishneh Torah*], and as long as a student of Ezra was alive, the remnants of the age of miracles continued. Shimon was also the *Cohen Gadol* / High Priest. The miracles that manifested in his physical presence included the following [Yerushalmi, *Yumah*, 6:3]: The western lamp of the Menorah in the Beis haMikdash remained permanently illuminated. A special blessing was present in the *Lechem haPanim* / the 'multifaceted' bread placed in the Beis haMikdash, and every Cohen who wanted a piece of it at the end of the week was able to receive a proper portion. Even if that portion was the minimum size, the Cohen would feel satiated from eating it.

Until the death of Shimon, there was a clear, linear progression of the *Mesorah* / tradition of the Torah transmitted personally from teacher to student. In addition, since the Torah was received in a context of direct revelation, prophecy, and 'received wisdom', there had been no arguments as to the interpretation of its laws. It was 'direct light', which is clear and unambiguous. It was one teaching from One Source, naturally unifying its recipients by nature of its reception. With the death of Shimon HaTzadik commenced the period of *Zugos* / pairs, 'two opinions'. From then on, there were always two or more schools of interpretation on any one issue. Wisdom was now revealed through a multiplicity of perspectives, dialogue, disagreement and debate. The first *Zug* / pair were students of Shimon haTzadik: Yossi the son of Yoezer, and Yossi the son of Yochanan.

Here is how Mishnah describes the transmission of Torah: "Moshe received the Torah from Sinai and gave it over to Yehoshua…to the Prophets, and the Prophets gave it over to the Men of the Great Assembly… Shimon haTzadik was among the last surviving members of the Great assembly… Antignos of Socho received the tradition from Shimon the Righteous…(and) Yossi the son of Yoezer…and Yossi the son of Yochanan…received the tradition from *them*" [*Avos*, 1:1-4].

Antignos was more a contemporary student or friend of Shimon [Shu't, *Tashbatz* 4, Siman 42]. Therefore, when the Mishnah says that Yossi ben Yoezer and Yossi ben Yochanan "received the tradition from them", "them" means that they were students of both Antignos and Shimon [*Rabbeinu Yonah*, Avos, 1:4. Tashbatz, ibid]. This is how, from the generation after Shimon, the full articulation and unfolding of the *Torah Shel Baal Peh* / Oral Torah began. This is the Torah of "them" — of multiple arguments and counter-arguments which gradually lead to a resolution and harmonization. Regarding the words of the great classic debaters, Shammai and Hillel, "These *and* these are the words of the living G-d" [*Eiruvin*, 13b]. This shows that the diversification of viewpoints at this stage was founded in an underlying unity, as such arguments were "for the sake of Heaven" [*Avos*, 5:2].

Once this process of holy debate was underway, however, contentious quarrels gained a foothold as well. Also, after some time, the students of Shammai and Hillel "did not sufficiently study and humbly receive the Torah from their teachers". As a result, *Machlokos* / arrogant disputes multiplied in Israel, to the point that the teachings of Shammai and Hillel became like "two Torahs" [*Sotah*, 47b. *Sanhedrin*, 88b].

From that period until our present day, all Jews agree on and practice the basics of the Mitzvos in a uniform way. However, there are still debates on many of the details. There are differences in opinion between Sefardim and Ashkenazim, for example, in whether one should sit or stand while putting on the hand Tefillin, and whether one should put on one or two Tefillin on the head. Within this specific divide, there are also differences between the opinion of the Aleppo Jews and the Turkish Jews, the German Jews and the Polish Jews. The Torah can now appear as 'dual', divided into different communities and opinions, or even 'broken', as it were.

This splintering within the Torah after the death of Ezra and Shimon began a new *Tzarah* / hardship within Klal Yisrael. Not only did different factions spring up, but also heretical groups, from the *Meshumadim* / those who denounced Torah and Mitzvos, to the *Tzedukim* / Sadducees, who accepted the Written Torah but rejected the Oral Torah; from the *Minim* / other Jewish heretics, to the *Notzrim* / Nazoreans who eventually separated from Klal Yisrael altogether. This inner dissension was, and continues to be, a most difficult Galus within Klal Yisrael. While the demise of Ezra did not 'have to' lead to this, the potential for it did begin with his death. There could have been holy arguments for the sake of Heaven, with an underlying harmony. But because the latter students did not sufficiently study or humbly receive the Torah from their teachers, the debates developed into more and more divisive arguments, angry misunderstandings and cutting of ties. For these reasons we mourn the death of Ezra and the end of prophecy. For these reasons we must awaken to Teshuvah during this period.

Now we can understand the severity of the fast of Teves, and why it is deeply relevant to us. This fast is a concentrated ritual response targeting all of the historical and existential 'openings' for negative potential which have lodged like thorns in the fabric of our collective experience. The piercing pain of these thorns is still felt today, as we are still ensconced in the Roman Exile, which includes all the other preceding exiles. We are still a splintered people, yearning to rebuild our original unity and harmony. But we can overcome these challenges when we all awaken, both individually and collectively.

May our Teshuvah be complete and whole. May we merit to see with our very own eyes, speedily in our days, the Unity of Hashem, revealed in the Unity of Torah, expressed and appreciated in the Unity of Klal Yisrael, actualized with the coming of Moshiach and the Unity of the World, signaling the end of all exiles, both human and Divine, *Amein*.

Other Books by the Author

RECLAIMING THE SELF
The Way of Teshuvah

Teshuvah is one of the great gifts of life. It speaks of a hope for a better today and empowers us to choose a brighter tomorrow. But what exactly is Teshuvah? How does it work? How can we undo our past and how do we deal with guilt? And what is healthy regret without eroding our self-esteem? In this fascinating and empowering book, the path for genuine transformation and a way to include all of our past in the powerful moment of the now, is explored and demonstrated.

THE MYSTERY OF KADDISH
Understanding the Mourner's Kaddish

The Mystery of Kaddish is an in-depth exploration into the Mourner's Prayer. Throughout Jewish history, there have been many rites and rituals associated with loss and mourning, yet none have prevailed quite like the Mourner's Kaddish Prayer, which has become the definitive ritual of mourning. The book explores the source of this prayer and deconstructs the meaning to better understand the grieving process and how the Kaddish prayer supports and uplifts the bereaved through their own personal journey to healing.

UPSHERNISH: The First Haircut
Exploring the Laws, Customs & Meanings
of a Boy's First Haircut

What is the meaning of Upsherin, the traditional celebration of a boy's first haircut at the age of three? Why is a boy's hair allowed to grow freely for his first three years? What is the deeper import of hair in all its lengths and varieties? What is the meaning of hair coverings? Includes a guide to conducting an Upsherin ceremony.

A BOND FOR ETERNITY
Understanding the Bris Milah

What is the Bris Milah – the covenant of circumcision? What does it represent, symbolize and signify? This book provides an in depth and sensitive review of this fundamental Mitzvah. In this little masterpiece of wisdom – profound yet accessible —the deeper meaning of this essential rite of passage and its eternal link to the Jewish people, is revealed and explored.

REINCARNATION AND JUDAISM
The Journey of the Soul

A fascinating analysis of the concept of Gilgul / Reincarnation. Dipping into the fountain of ancient wisdom and modern understanding, this book addresses and answers such basic questions as: What is reincarnation? Why does it occur? And how does it affect us personally?

INNER RHYTHMS
The Kabbalah of MUSIC

Exploring the inner dimension of sound and music, and particularly, how music permeates all aspects of life. The topics range from Deveikus/Unity and Yichudim/Unifications, to the more personal issues, such as Simcha/Happiness and Marirus/ sadness.

MEDITATION AND JUDAISM
Exploring the Jewish Meditative Paths

A comprehensive work encompassing the entire spectrum of Jewish thought, from the sages of the Talmud and the early Kabbalists to the modern philosophers and Chassidic masters. This book is both a scholarly, in-depth study of meditative practices, and a practical, easy to follow guide for any person interested in meditating the Jewish way.

TOWARD THE INFINITE

A book focusing exclusively on the Chassidic approach to meditation known as Hisbonenus. Encompassing the entire meditative experience, it takes the reader on a comprehensive and engaging journey through this unique practice. The book explores the various states of consciousness that a person encounters in the course of the meditation, beginning at a level of extreme self-awareness and concluding with a state of total non-awareness.

THIRTY – TWO GATES OF WISDOM
Awakening through Kabbalah

Kabbalah holds the secrets to a path of conscious awareness. In this compact book, 32 key concepts of Kabbalah are explored and their value in opening the gates of perception are demonstrated.

THE PURIM READER
The Holiday of Purim Explored

With a Persian name, a masquerade dress code and a woman as the heroine, Purim is certainly unusual amongst the Jewish holidays. Most people are very familiar with the costumes, Megilah and revelry, but are mystified by their significance. This book offers a glimpse into the hidden world of Purim, uncovering these mysteries and offering a deeper understanding of this unique holiday.

EIGHT LIGHTS
8 Meditations for Chanukah

What is the meaning and message of Chanukah? What is the spiritual significance of the Lights of the Menorah? What are the Lights telling us? What is the deeper dimension of the Dreidel? Rav Pinson, with his trademark deep learning and spiritual sensitivity guides us through eight meditations relating to the Lights of the Menorah, the eight days of Chanukah, and a fascinating exploration of the symbolism and structure of the Dreidel. Includes a detailed how-to guide for lighting the Chanukah Menorah.

THE IYYUN HAGADAH
An Introduction to the Haggadah

In this beautifully written introduction to Passover and the Haggadah, we are guided through the major themes of Passover and the Seder night. This slim text, addresses the important questions, such as: What is the big deal of Chametz? What are we trying to achieve through conducting a Seder? What's with all that stuff on the Seder Plate? And most importantly, how is this all related to freedom?

PASSPORT TO KABBALAH
A Journey of Inner Transformation

Life is a journey full of ups and downs, inside-outs, and unexpected detours. There are times when we think we know exactly where we want to be headed, and other times when we are so lost we don't even know where we are. This slim book provides readers with a passport of sorts to help them through any obstacles along their path of self-refinement, reflection, and self-transformation.

THE FOUR SPECIES
The Symbolism of the Lulav & Esrog

The Four Species have inspired countless commentaries and traditions and intrigued scholars and mystics alike. In this little masterpiece of wisdom both profound and practical - the deep symbolic roots and nature of the Four Species are explored. The Na'anuim, or ritual of the Lulav movement, is meticulously detailed and Kavanos,, are offered for use with the practice. Includes an illustrated guide to the Lulav Movements.

THE BOOK OF LIFE AFTER LIFE

What is a soul? What happens to us after we physically die?

What is consciousness, and can it survive without a physical brain?

Can we remember our past lives?

Do near-death experiences prove immortality?

What is Gan Eden? Resurrection?

Exploring the possibility of surviving death, the near-death experience and a glimpse into what awaits us after this life.

(This book is an updated and expanded version of the book; Jewish Wisdom of the Afterlife)

THE GARDEN OF PARADOX:
The Essence of Non - Dual Kabbalah

This book is a Primer on the Essential Philosophy of Kabbalah presented as a series of 3 conversations, revealing the mysteries of Creator, Creation and Consciousness. With three representational students, embodying respectively, the philosopher, the activist and the mystic, the book, tackles the larger questions of life. Who is G-d? Who am I? Why do I exist? What is my purpose in this life? Written in clear and concise prose, the text, gently guides the reader towards making sense of life's paradoxes and living meaningfully.

BREATHING & QUIETING THE MIND

Achieving a sense of self-mastery and inner freedom demands that we gain a measure of hegemony over our thoughts. We learn to choose out thoughts so that we are not at the mercy of whatever belches up to the mind. Through quieting the mind and conscious breathing we can slow the onrush of anxious, scattered thinking and come to a deeper awareness of the interconnectedness of all of life.

Source texts are included in translation, with how-to-guides for the various practices.

VISUALIZATION AND IMAGERY:
Harnessing the Power of our Mind's Eye

We assume that what we see with our eyes is absolute. Yet, beyond our ability to choose what we see, we have the ability to choose how we see. This directly translates into how we experience life. In a world saturated with visual imagery, our senses are continuously assaulted with Kelipa/empty/fantasy imagery that we would not necessarily choose. These images can negatively affect our relationship with ourselves, with the world around us, and with the Divine. This volume seeks to show us how we can alter that which we observe through harnessing the power of our mind's eye, the inner sanctum of our imagination. We thus create a new way to see and experience the world. This book teaches us how to utilize visualization and imagery as a way to develop our spiritual sensitivity and higher intuition, and ultimately achieve Deveikus/Unity with Hashem.

THE POWER OF CHOICE:
A Practical Guide to Conscious Living

It is the essential premise of this book that we hold the key to unlock many of the gates that seem closed to us and keep us from living our fullest life. That key we all hold is the power to choose. The Power of Choice is the primary tool that we have at our disposal to impact the world and effect change within our own lives. We often give up this power to outside forces such as the market, media, politicians or peer pressure; or to internal forces that often function beyond our conscious control such as ego, anger, lust, greed or jealousy. Making conscious, compassionate and creative decisions is the cornerstone of living a mature and meaningful life.

MYSTIC TALES FROM THE EMEK HAMELECH

Mystic Tales of the Emek HaMelech, is a wondrous and inspiring collection of stories culled from the Emek HaMelech. Emek HaMelech, from which these stories have been taken, (as well as its author) is a bit of a mystery. But like all good mysteries, it is one worth investigating. In this spirit the present volume is being offered to the general public in the merit and memory of its saintly author, as well as in the hopes of introducing a vital voice of deeper Torah teaching and tradition to a contemporary English speaking audience

---

INNER WORLDS OF JEWISH PRAYER
A Guide to Develop and Deepen the Prayer Experience

While much attention has been paid to the poetry, history, theology and contextual meaning of the prayers, the intention of this work is to provide a guide to finding meaning and effecting transformation through the prayer experience itself.

Explore: *What happens when we pray? *How do we enter the mind-state of prayer? *Learning to incorporate the body into the prayers. *Discover techniques to enhance and deepen prayer and make it a transformative experience.

This empowering and inspiring text, demonstrates how through proper mindset, preparation and dedication, the experience of prayer can be deeply transformative and ultimately, life-altering.

WRAPPED IN MAJESTY
Tefillin - Exploring the Mystery

Tefillin, the black boxes and leather straps that are worn during prayer, are curiously powerful and mysterious. Within the inky black boxes lie untold secrets. In this profound, passionate and thought-provoking text, the multi-dimensional perspectives of Tefillin are explored and revealed. Magically weaving together all levels of Torah including the Peshat (literal observation), to Remez (allegorical), to Derush, (homiletic), to Sod (hidden) into one beautiful tapestry. Inspirational and instructive, Wrapped in Majesty: Tefillin, will make putting on the Tefillin more meaningful and inspiring.

THE SPIRAL OF TIME:
A 12 Part Series on the Months of the Year.

Now Available!

THE SPIRAL OF TIME:
Unraveling the Yearly Cycle

Many centuries ago, the Sages of Israel were the foremost authority in the fields of both astronomical calculation and astrological wisdom, including the deeper interpretations of the cycles and seasons. Over time, this wisdom became hidden within the esoteric teachings of the Torah, and as a result was known only to students and scholars of the deepest depths of the tradition. More recently, the great teachers, from R.Yitzchak Luria (the Arizal) to the Baal Shem Tov, taught that as the world approaches the Era of Redemption, it is a Mitzvah / spiritual obligation to broadly reveal this wisdom.

"The Spiral of Time" is volume 1 is a series of 12 books, and serves as an introductory book to the basic concepts and nature of the Hebrew calendar and explores the special day of Rosh Chodesh.

THE MONTH OF SHEVAT: ELEVATING EATING
& The Holiday of Tu b'Shevat

Each month of the year radiates with a distinct Divine energy and thus unique opportunities for growth, *Tikkun* and illumination. According to the deeper teachings of the Torah, all of these distinct qualities, opportunities and natural phenomena correspond to a certain data set. That is, the nature of each month is elucidated by a specific letter of the Aleph Beis, a tribe, verse, human sense, and so forth. The month of Shevat is particularly connected to food and our relationship to bodily intake. During this month we celebrate Tu b'Shevat, the New Year of the Tree, and aspire to create a proper and physically/emotionally/spiritually healthy relationship with food.

THE MONTH OF IYYAR: EVOLVING THE SELF
& The Holiday of LAG B'OMER

The month of IYYAR is the second month of the spring, a month that connects the Redemption from Egypt in Nissan with the Revelation of Torah in Sivan. The Chai/ Eighteenth day of the

Month is the day we celebrate the Rashbi (Rabbi Shimon Bar Yochai) and the revealing of the hidden aspects of the Torah. This is the 'Holiday' of Lag b'Omer. The book explores the unique quality of this special month, a month that has a Mitzvah of counting the Omer every day. In addition, the book explores the roots and significance of the mystical 'holiday' of Lag b'Omer. Including the customs & Practices of Lag b'Omer, such as, bonfires, bows & arrows, parades, Upsherin, and more.

THE MONTHS OF TAMUZ/AV:
Embracing Brokenness, Transforming Darkness
The Three Weeks: From the 17th of Tamuz until the 9th of Av & Tu b'Av

Each month and season of the year, radiates with distinct Divine qualities and unique opportunities for growth and Tikkun. The summer month of Tamuz and Av contain the longest and hottest days of the year. The raised temperature is indicative of a corresponding spiritual heat, a time of harsher judgement and potential destruction, such as the destruction of the first and second Beis HaMikdash, which began on the 17th of Tamuz and culminated on the 9th & 10th of Av. A few days later, on Tu b'Av, the darkness is transformed and reveals the greatest light and possibility for new life. During these summer months of Tamuz and Av we embrace our brokenness so that we can heal and transform darkness into light.

SOUND AND VIBRATION
Tuning into the Echoes of Creation

Through our perception of sound and vibration we internalize the world around us. What we hear, and how we process that hearing, has a profound impact on how we experience life. What we hear can empower us or harm us. A defining human capacity is to harness the power sound — through speech, dialogue, and song, and through listening to others. Hearing is primary dimension of our existence. In fact, as a fetus our ears were the first fully operating sensory organs to develop.

This book will guide you in methods of utilizing the power of sound and vibration to heal and maintain mental, emotional and spiritual health, to fine-tune your Midos and even to guide you into deeper levels of Deveikus / conscious unity with Hashem. The vibratory patterns of the Aleph-Beis are particularly useful portals into our deeper conscious selves. Through chanting and deep listening, we can use the letters and sounds to shift our very mindset, to induce us into a state of presence and spiritual elevation.

THE SECRET OF THE MIKVAH
Waters of Transformation

A Mikvah is a pool of water used for the purpose of ritual immersion; a place where one moves from a state of Tumah / impurity, blockage and 'death', to a place of Teharah/ purity, fluidity and life.

This text delves into the depths of wisdom to reveal the secret transformative power of the Mikvah and water. Exploring the nature of Mikvah from multi-dimensional perspectives, from the Peshat (literal observation and Halacha), to the Remez (allegorical), the Derush, (homiletical and philosophical), to the Sod (hidden, Kabbalah and Chassidus). This empowering, insightful and inspirational text, demonstrates how the Mikvah experience can be truly transformative and life-altering.

The text also includes various particle Kavanos / intentions that can be used when immersing in the Mikvah.

www.ingramcontent.com/pod-product-compliance
Lightning Source LLC
Chambersburg PA
CBHW071410160426
42813CB00085B/954